LOST AT THE FRONTIER

LOST AT THE FRONTIER

U.S. Science and Technology Policy Adrift

Deborah Shapley/Rustum Roy

Philadelphia

Published by

iSi PRESS® A Subsidiary of the
Institute for Scientific Information®
3501 Market St., University City Science Center, Philadelphia, PA 19104 U.S.A.

Library of Congress Cataloging in Publication Data

Shapley, Deborah, 1945–
  Lost at the frontier.

  Bibliography: p.
  Includes index.
  1. Science and state — United States. 2. Technology and state — United States.
  I. Roy, Rustum. II. Title.
  Q127.U6S48 1985   338.97306   84-22592
  ISBN 0-89495-041-X
  ISBN 0-89495-042-8 (pbk.)

Portions of Edwin H. Land's response are taken from the Charles F. Kettering
Award address, delivered 17 June 1965. It first appeared in "Selected Papers on
Industry" published in 1983 by Polaroid Corporation. It is reprinted here with per-
mission of Polaroid.

Printed in the United States of America
90 89 88 87 86 85   8 7 6 5 4 3 2 1

Contents

Preface

Although we work in different professions (one of us is a senior materials scientist and lab administrator, the other a science journalist) and in different cities, we felt compelled to put forward this essay from a common fear that our country's benefits from science—in the sense that most people think of the benefits of science, i.e., more inventions, more jobs, healthy companies, a better quality of life, and a more favorable balance of trade—cannot be taken for granted. Already, much of the nation's private, public, and industrial life depends on science and technology; many are predicting a quantum jump in the extent of our dependence on them in the future; some even predict another science-based industrial revolution. Nonetheless, the two of us have doubts that the U.S. science profession, as presently constituted, will serve that revolution as well as it should.

The public image of science these days is upbeat; laymen think of science as an "endless frontier" (to borrow the phrase Vannevar Bush used in a famous 1945 report that helped to shape our present science profession) that will automatically bring more inventions, more jobs, etc., in its wake. What has struck us so forcefully is the extent to which many scientists we both know are reluctant to get into the business of invention, or creating new industries, or helping with societal problems such as education. Many believe what we consider the mythology that science must be divorced from applications, that science serves the nation best when it is done only for science's sake. The profession, we agreed, tends to cut science off from its natural linkages to technology and society at large; thus, it has cast itself adrift on its own endless frontier.

Though of long standing concern, this question of the severance of ties between basic science and applications has not been central to the postwar science policy debate, and we quickly realized our principal ideas would be seen as controversial. So, to help set them in context, we invited a number of distinguished people, each of whom is important to the current science policy debate, to read our essay and respond with written comments to be included in this volume. Our model was *The New Liberal Arts*, a 1981 report of the Alfred P. Sloan Foundation which put forward the equally controversial idea that liberal arts, if it is to remain the carrier of our core culture from the Trojans to the Victorians, should include computers and applied math (an idea which is congenial with the holistic spirit of our principal themes). The Sloan Foundation had recognized the possible storm its proposal might stir, and it invited comments from people on all sides of this question. The success of that volume prompted the Sloan Foundation to encourage us to try the same formula again.

We were surprised and delighted with the number of those invited who accepted, and with the very high quality of their comments. They are, in our view, at least as interesting as the main essay. We are also grateful to the Sloan Foundation, which helped make their contributions possible. With all this assistance, we hope the result of this project will be constructive discussion about how U.S. science can become *un*lost at its endless frontier.

Acknowledgments

Both authors acknowledge with gratitude the support of the Alfred P. Sloan Foundation which made possible the research and writing of this book. One of us was supported directly (D.S.) and the other indirectly (R.R.) through the opportunity to be a Science Fellow at the Brookings Institution in 1982–1983. We are grateful to the Brookings Institution and its staff for providing a stimulating environment for this and related work. We want to thank Joshua Lerner for his research assistance and Pam Harris, Vera Poling, and Nelly Ledesma, who helped in manuscript preparation.

We benefited enormously from the advice of several individuals: Philip H. Abelson, Jordan J. Baruch, Justin Bloom, Edward J. Burger, Arthur M. Diness, Robert A. Frosch, N. Bruce Hannay, Vilma Hunt, Daniel S. Greenberg, Jack Goldman, Willis H. Shapley, Bruce L. R. Smith, John Sherman, Lewis Thomas, and Ernst U. von Weizsäcker, as well as others who were interviewed in the course of our research. Special thanks go to William O. Baker, George Brown, Pat Choate, Harry C. Gatos, Walter A. Hahn, James R. Killian, Jr., Edwin H. Land, F. James Rutherford, and Eric A. Walker, who took the time from busy schedules to provide the written responses to our essay which appear at the end of this volume. Obviously, none of those we interviewed is in any way responsible for the opinions expressed in this book.

1

U.S. Science Adrift

THE IDEA OF THE frontier has been central to American history and thought. The colonies' frontier status shaped their social and political character in the seventeenth and eighteenth centuries: the nation was shaped in the nineteenth century in large part by the expansion west. In the twentieth century, as the geographical frontiers closed, other frontiers emerged; among them was U.S. science, which was transformed by the two world wars and the influx of refugee scientists from Europe. So in 1944, when President Roosevelt asked Vannevar Bush, who had led the wartime scientific effort, for a plan for postwar science, it is hardly surprising that Bush invoked this old and powerful idea to explain his plan, and called his report to the President, delivered in July 1945, *Science—The Endless Frontier.*[1]

The report argued that organized exploration of this hinterland, if supported by the federal government, could bring both intellectual adventure and rich economic rewards to the nation. And for twenty years *Science—The Endless Frontier* seemed remarkably prescient. U.S. science enjoyed a flowering like none it had had before—or any other nation's science had had. U.S. scientists garnered the lion's share of Nobel Prizes; our large, well-funded, and diversified science effort was the envy of the world. U.S. technology also flourished, as did the major industries such as electronics,

1

chemicals, plastics, and pharmaceuticals — many of which were emerging at the war's end.

But now, things seem to have gone sour. The commanding lead of the postwar years has been dissipated. In many fields, U.S. technology no longer leads. Some science-based technology, such as supercomputers, is racing neck and neck with that of Japan, and will be for the foreseeable future. U.S. science, after a decade of level or declining budgets followed by slow increases, is under strain too. Several explanations have been proposed for the current problems: lack of enough federal money, too much regulation, and so on. In our view, the problems are deeper. They stem from the structure and values of the postwar science system that was based in part on *Science—The Endless Frontier*. The problems were intrinsic to the system, but masked by two decades of prosperity in the 1950s and 1960s. In our view, today's declining high-technology trade balance, the fragility of U.S. industries, and the serious lack of public understanding of science show that the United States has not exploited the frontier of science as well as it might have. Moreover, basic science itself faces serious difficulties, even with federal funds finally starting to rise (see Figure 1).

This essay is an experiment in science criticism. It expresses our jointly held opinions: one of us is a senior practicing materials scientist and laboratory administrator; the other is a science journalist. It does not try to be definitive or comprehensive, and it cannot discuss the detailed problems of each sector, from biotechnology to materials science to automotive research, because the problems vary from field to field. It falls, we hope, between science journalism and conventional science policy analysis. We are here only presenting a case, based on our discussions with a number of scientific managers in government, industry, and universities. We believe our empirical approach is as necessary and useful as the reductionist, pseudo-scientific study of details that characterizes much science policy literature. The readers, of course, will judge for themselves.

The reader should imagine that, in our respective careers, we have been to the theater, have talked about the show, and have written a review of it. And just as no theater director would use a reviewer's comments as a verbatim script for the next night's performance, our recommendations are not precise prescriptions. But practicing scientists and those who make research policy in universities, industry, and federal and state government should welcome reviews from sympathetic spectators. For one obstacle to a candid debate about what is wrong with U.S. science has been the vanity that the study of science, and the management of it, must be "scientific." We think good science is a creative activity, like good theater, art, or even sports. Science supported by the public purse is just as open for serious scrutiny as a show that sells tickets to the public. We hope that our experiment will stimulate others and liven up the debate about the future of the science profession.

I

The touchpoint for this essay is the report Roosevelt commissioned as World War II was winding down and the contributions of scientists to the war effort were becoming known in and out of government. The moment was ripe to plan for postwar science. Bush, responding to the President, asked many key figures in the science community to sit on committees that would write individual reports to answer Roosevelt's query. (Four such committees were established: one on a program to continue the work in medicine and related sciences, chaired by W. W. Palmer of Columbia University; one on the proper roles of public and private sectors, headed by Isaiah Bowman, President of Johns Hopkins University; one on discovering and developing scientific manpower, headed by Henry Allen Moe, Chairman of the John Simon Guggenheim Memorial Foundation; and one on the lifting of military secrecy, headed by Irvin Stewart, Executive Secretary of the Office of Scientific Research and Development.) Bush had managed the wartime scientific effort through the Office of Scientific Research and Development (OSRD), and one more report to the President was hardly a chore. Except that this one would discuss, in effect, his and his colleagues' future.

Nine months later, on 4 July 1945, Bush reported back to the President. "We did not take five years," he wrote later, "because within our committees there has been an extraordinary consensus."[2]

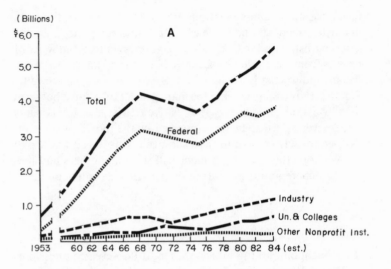

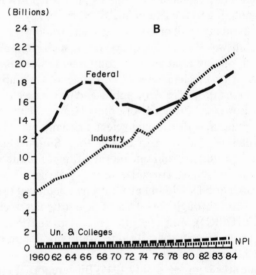

Figures 1A, 1B, and 1C Key changes in U.S. research and development funding which pose serious challenges to U.S. science.

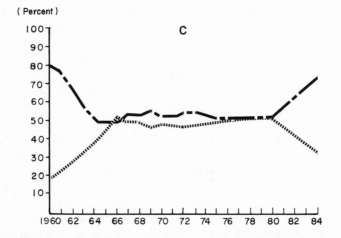

(Percent)

Figure 1A Government and industry funding of basic research, by sector, 1953–1984, showing the change from an era of steep growth in the 1950s and 1960s, the decline of the 1970s, and the modest increases since. Data in constant 1972 dollars. (SOURCE: National Patterns of Science and Technology Resources 1984, National Science Foundation, NSF 84-311, 1984, Appendix Table 7, p. 33.)

Figure 1B Total U.S. research and development funding, 1960–1984. This shows the same pattern for the overall effort, of steep growth, decline, and slow increases. It also shows the dramatic increase in industry spending which, as we shall see, is virtually all in the areas of hardware development (one factor being the recent military buildup) and near-term product development. Data in constant 1972 dollars. (SOURCE: *Science Indicators 1982*, figure 2-5, p. 44, and appendix table 2-3, p. 235; also National Patterns of Science and Technology Resources 1984, Appendix Table 5, p. 32.)

Figure 1C A third significant change is in the shifting percentage of the total federal effort devoted to military (– – –), as opposed to civilian (----), research and development, shown here. In 1960 the military share stood at 80 percent; the early 1960s were characterized by rapid growth in the civilian share; most of the recent increases in federal R&D are in the military sector. Overall recent growth has masked the sharp decline in the civilian share, the share which is perhaps most important in assisting future U.S. industrial competitiveness in high technology products. (SOURCE: *Science Indicators 1982*, Figure 2-14, p. 52.)

Was it born of a sense of national purpose? Atomic weapons had not yet been detonated. The wartime scientists were not so famous as they would be in a few months after Hiroshima and Nagasaki. They felt they must put their case strongly, to skeptical officials in the executive branch and Congress.

The report was, in many ways, a propaganda document that advertised the great benefits that could flow from science in order to persuade the government to support it. American science had been poor between the wars; at that time the government showed no interest despite some scientists' pleas. But now, with the banner of their wartime achievements to wave, the scientists were trying again. So the report reflects the world Bush and his colleagues hoped to create for themselves when they returned to their campuses and laboratories at the war's close. But besides being propaganda, the document reflects the group's world view, its view of the relations between science and technology, its assumptions and beliefs.

The report argued that science had helped the United States and its allies win the war and could be equally critical in peace. To create a strong, peacetime scientific effort in the United States, it said, the federal government should step in with generous and stable funding for research, especially basic research in universities. It proposed the creation of a National Research Foundation, run by a board of scientists from universities and industry, which would support military, medical, and physical science research. The board would make national policy for research and scientific education by advising "the executive and legislative branches of Government as to the policies and budgets" of all science-related agencies. The four appendices, on medical research, the structure of the proposed Foundation, policies for scientific manpower, and the declassification of scientific information, spelled out the details of how to move science to a peacetime footing.

In rereading the Bush report from our respective viewpoints, we were struck by how selectively it has been used despite its reputation as the blueprint for what came after. Much of the report's call for federal support of science was carried out. Although Truman vetoed a bill in 1947 that would have created a "National Research Foundation" on the Bush report's model, in 1950 he finally agreed to create the National Science Foundation (NSF). The NSF had, however, only a small part of the total mandate Bush outlined for his proposed National Research Foundation. As OSRD phased out, the Office of Naval Research took over sponsorship of research at many top universities. When the Atomic Energy Commission was established in 1946, it assumed a big role in supporting physics research. Medical researchers elected to expand their own government agency, the National Institute of Health, rather than cast their lot with the physical scientists and the proposed foundation. Even when the NSF got started in 1951, it never did become a formulator of *national* science policy, or a sponsor of military research, or the framer of national education policy in the sciences. All these postwar research organizations can trace their ancestry to the successful plea made by *Science—The Endless Frontier.*

Yet although the Bush report has become sanctified as the charter for federal support of basic research, we shall see that it talked about many other things besides basic research with equal emphasis. It does indeed talk about basic research and the need for federal support for science in universities, because this had not existed before in peacetime. Such support would be new — whereas the other components discussed in the report as equally essential to postwar prosperity already existed, such as the applied science done in government laboratories and in industry. Contrary to the mythology that grew up about the report later, it does not treat basic research in a vacuum, but as one of the steps in a chain of endeavor that leads to industrial advance, better public health, and stronger national defense. It is noteworthy that the report's authors, by 1945, had had experience with many of these steps in the chain, first-hand.

Our view is that in the since-neglected passages of *Science— The Endless Frontier,* which still ring true, lies the key to today's troubles and to why U.S. science seems lost at the endless frontier Bush spoke of. Where do we go from here? some spokesmen for science have been asking. The answers they offer are often monotonous: Science needs more money. There is too much government interference. The public does not understand science's specialness.

In our view, the Bush report contains a much broader message that was ignored for the most part in the evolution of postwar science institutions. This message concerned its authors' own experience with the *interconnectedness* of basic research with other parts of the process, along a spectrum from basic research to applied science, to engineering, to technology, to public, national needs. The people who came after Bush and his colleagues (in this essay we shall call them the "followers of Bush," because they followed him chronologically although not in spirit), who set up the system and trained the current generation of scientists, narrowed the definition of what science is, how it should be done, and why. Unwittingly, they set in motion a chain of events that today has isolated much of the U.S. basic research community, especially many university researchers, from the larger problems of the country.

Moreover, by creating in the basic scientists trained in the system a belief that they were *entitled* to federal support *automatically*, as a birthright, they created in the profession a morbid preoccupation with the federal science budget and winning the next grant — which preoccupies many of them often more than doing creative work. We agree with Gerald Holton's remark that any profession, including science, "can regain its moral authority only if it is perceived as serving both truth and the public interest."[3] Scientists have always claimed to serve the truth. But today's crop (unlike the Bush generation whose values were shaped by the 1930s and their wartime public service) no longer see their profession as having much to do with the broad national interest, the problems of the steel industry, the balance of trade, or the ignorance of the ordinary citizens who foot the bill through their taxes. To Congress they promise that their research will bring prosperity. But to each other they often abjure such mundane goals and want to see science funded for the sake of perpetuating itself.

So, says our theater review, it was a good script and a fine cast, and the patrons spared no expense on sets and costumes. But the director fouled it up by letting that glittering diva, Basic Research, hog the stage. The postwar system, established in the name of fueling the engines of economic advance and helping humanity, focused on part of the overall task, providing federal research funds for high science — that is, research at the purest end of the spectrum. Of course, the government funded certain applied missions in defense, nuclear power, and space. But the core of the science system, its *raison d'être*, was not Bush's sweeping vision but a limited one: federal support for that part of the profession who were believed to be at its apex — scientists, in universities, pursuing research having no application.

What was lost, in a word, was the importance of applied science and engineering, and something else that we shall call *purposive basic research*, i.e., research of a fundamental nature that is done with a general application in mind, like Charles H. Townes' discovery of the maser while working on microwave transmission for Bell Laboratories, or most biomedical research. All of these — engineering, applied science, and purposive basic research — are important members of the cast. They are critical in the utilization of scientific discoveries and often provoke scientific advances. Yet they are, in our present science culture, second class citizens. The result is well expressed by John Steele, the Scottish-born Director of the prestigious Woods Hole Oceanographic Laboratory. The United States, Steele comments, is very good at immediate product development and very good at basic research in our elite universities and a few industrial laboratories. But we are weak at the parts of the process that lie in between. A big part of what is troubling U.S. science, then, is the same problem troubling U.S. industry (for industry has neglected purposive basic research too, although this is changing, as we will discuss in Chapter 3): lack of high-level attention to and intelligent management of the middle parts of the science-to-innovation spectrum.

Applied science historically had been the country's great strength. The country's development in the nineteenth century had been based on Yankee ingenuity and harnessing known science to technology and to practical ends. Matthew Fontaine Maury, the first Superintendent of the Naval Observatory was considered a great scientist, because he had persuaded hundreds of ship's captains to fill in and return to him standard reporting logs. These built up progressively more complete and accurate editions of Maury's *Wind and Current Directions*, the indispensable source of wind, temperature, and current data for mariners worldwide.[4]

The Morrill (1862 and 1890) and Hatch (1887) Acts contributed

a distinctly American model to publicly supported science by establishing the land-grant colleges (which were cited as models for
future U.S. science institutions in Bush's report). The land-grant
colleges were for children of farmers, artisans, and the middle class
generally to educate them in agriculture and the mechanical arts.
They offered science, applied science, technology, and training.
They offered a system for *coupling* knowledge with the people who
would apply it in the field. Their knowledge base was not exclusively basic science, nor would it be they who would later crack
the genetic code. Their *forte* was empirical genetics; moreover, they
brought together on a regional basis knowledge of mechanization,
local crop specialization, know-how, and new knowledge, and so
turned the frontier into a granary.[5] In Chapter 3 we will discuss
how this system remained continuously innovative for a century,
and its current decline. For the old agricultural research system remains the paradigm of the conditions we think are essential for
innovative, productive science that functions, as Bush said, as part
of a team. Indeed, part of the evidence that the postwar U.S. science
system evolved away from Bush's ideas is that, whereas he held
up agriculture as the model for postwar science, his followers
preferred pure physics as theirs. Agricultural science has been low
in the pecking order ever since, having never recovered the prestige
it then lost to high-energy physics.

Thus, American technology evolved for the most part without
reference to high science. Josiah Willard Gibbs, a major figure in
thermodynamics, mineralogists Benjamin Silliman and James D.
Dana, and physicist Joseph Henry worked at the cutting edge of
science only by reference to Europe. Henry Ford, Andrew Carnegie,
and the Wright brothers all succeeded without benefit of science
clergy.[6]

From the perspective of 1945 it was possible to argue that this
had changed, that U.S. industry relied more and more on science-
based technology. Critical advances in physics and mathematics
in the 1920s and 1930s had brought a scientific revolution: the spill-
over came in the development of nuclear weapons, radar, and later
in computers. The emerging chemicals and plastics industries were
arguably more science-based than their counterparts of the century before, and scientists felt free to have their profession take the
credit for having fueled the twentieth-century industrial revolution.[7]

The wartime leaders of science could argue — and their followers made it dogma — that without advances in basic physical sciences there would have been neither radar nor the atomic bomb. These arguments were historically misleading. The success of these advances resulted from many things besides Werner Heisenberg's tinkering in his university lab in Germany or Heinrich Hertz's experiments. The development of the atomic bomb and radar illustrates the interconnectedness of basic science with engineering and the other parts of the spectrum; the bomb "flowed" no more automatically from the discovery of fission than Alexander Fleming's notice in 1928 that his bacterial cultures had been contaminated by penicillin mold led automatically to the dispensing of the penicillin vaccine to troops in World War II.

Derek deSolla Price, the late Yale historian of science, illustrated this point vividly in a lecture he gave to the American Association for the Advancement of Science in 1983.

> It has often been supposed, on no real basis but assertion, that science can in some mysterious way be applied to make technology. Quite commonly it is said that there is a great chain of being that runs from basic science to applied science and thence to development in a natural and orderly progression that takes one from the core of science to technology.

Price disputed this view vigorously.

> The arrow of causality historically is largely from the technology to the science.

To support his case, he cited none other than Galileo's discovery of the moons of Jupiter which brought the Copernican revolution in astronomy. It all happened because of the unrelated development of eyeglasses for thirteenth-century monks copying manuscripts. This led to the development of the glass lathe in the sixteenth century and the construction of thick concave lenses as a curiosity for artists seeking unusual perspectives. When two lens grinders from the Low Countries were peddling pairs of such lenses as a spy tool to the military, they consulted Galileo ("an uncommonly aggressive would-be consultant," Price noted). He, in turn, pointed them upwards to look at the night sky.

The discovery of current electricity and electrolysis by Galvani and Volta around 1800, Price added, occurred when they fiddled with an electric machine in an attempt to sense the life force in the back legs of a frog. This—more than the theories of Lavoisier—transformed alchemy into modern chemistry, Price maintained. Moreover, biology relied on the textile industry for dyes to stain tissue; the cloud chamber that made modern physics possible came about when a mountaineering buff named C. T. R. Wilson tried to simulate clouds in a laboratory full of Rutherford's radioactivity experiments. Formal theorists of science, nonetheless, have ignored these tinkerings. Our arrangements for science and technology, Price said, put the theoretician first and treat "the people with brains in their fingertips"—the real makers of scientific revolutions—as servants.[8]

This same false mythology has trumpeted the development of the atomic bomb as the result of pure science. But at Los Alamos during the war, Robert Oppenheimer put his team of scientists to work on applied tasks: George Kistiakowsky worked on explosives for the bomb's gun, John von Neumann worked out a large compression theory to predict the explosion, and so on. In hindsight, Oppenheimer may be viewed as a chain-smoking dreamy-eyed genius, but at Los Alamos he was literally knocking the heads of his researchers together to get the job done on time.[9] (Indeed, the real lesson of the Manhattan project for today is what can be accomplished when the highest quality, most basic scientists are organized and motivated to work on applications, of which more later.)

Similarly, while radar could not have been invented without Hertz and Guglielmo Marconi, the outstanding feature of the story is not that their discoveries trickled into the applied arena, but how the imperative of the war pulled the development of the technology. The achievements during the war of the Radiation Laboratory at the Massachusetts Institute of Technology (M.I.T.) were no mean feats: at least one assessment credits the laboratory with having been far more inventive and productive because of its freewheeling character. There would have been fewer inventions if the job had been turned over to a conventional military organization, such as the Navy. An important footnote is that some of the sets built at the Radiation Laboratory were shipped to the battlefield for combat use.[10]

Historically, then, many cases most often cited as proving the primacy of undirected basic research show the opposite. Instead, often there was a clear long-range goal, an intermingling of basic research and applications. The scientific leaders of that time valued applications and inventions. A touching illustration came during the war when Albert Einstein was asked to serve as a consultant by a lieutenant in the Navy Bureau of Ordnance's Research and Development Division. The discoverer of special and general relativity, who had been mobbed by cheering crowds when he first visited America in 1921, happily worked for $25 per day on problems such as whether a torpedo's detonation should be initiated in the front or back end, under the orders of a lieutenant. In his job interview Einstein complained: "People think I am interested only in theory, and not in anything practical. This is not true. I was working in the Patent Office in Zurich and I participated in the development of many inventions, the gyroscope, too."[11]

It is noteworthy that Einstein's historical image, like that of Oppenheimer, has been recast as a dreamy scientist in sandals, and references to his passion for inventing things are few and far between. The new memorial statue erected by the National Academy of Sciences on its grounds in Washington, for example, includes no mention of the practical side of his achievements. This may say something about the preconceptions of those doing the memorializing!

II

In 1945, Vannevar Bush, James B. Conant, President of Harvard, Frank B. Jewett, President of the Academy and Chairman of the Board of Bell Telephone Laboratories, and Karl T. Compton, President of M.I.T. — the "big four" of the wartime science effort — stood at a unique moment in U.S. history. Science-based technology had succeeded as never before; and the forced march in the field of health had proved that science could save people, as well as destroy them. American industry had generated unparalleled momentum: new chemicals and plastics were emerging; the automotive and aircraft industries were poised to jump into expanded civilian markets. Yet the European universities, where many of the wartime group had trained, were now in ruins. Was the United States too practical a place for high science to take root? Bush adopted the frontier metaphor to persuade people that there was something American about high science. His report said:

> It has been basic United States policy that Government should foster the opening of new frontiers. It opened the seas to clipper ships and furnished land for pioneers. Although these frontiers have more or less disappeared, the frontier of science remains. It is in keeping with the American tradition — one which has made the United States great — that new frontiers shall be made accessible for development by all American citizens.

And later:

> We can no longer count on ravaged Europe as a source of fundamental knowledge. In the past we have devoted much of our best efforts to the application of such knowledge which has been discovered abroad. In the future we must pay increased attention to discovering this knowledge for ourselves.[12]

Where would new knowledge come from? the report asked. Industry cannot be counted on to produce it, for industry takes too short-term a view of what products are needed. Nonprofit institutions, which had done much for research in the past, seemed to be pulling out. Government must step in and foster this knowledge in its own laboratories and in the place knowledge grows best — the universities. The report undertook to define this item, "basic research," and the requirements for its health. In a classic passage, much quoted by Bush's followers, it said:

> Basic research is performed without thought of practical ends. It results in general knowledge and an understanding of nature and its laws. This general knowledge provides the means of answering a large number of important practical problems, though it may not give a complete, specific answer to any one of them. The scientist doing basic research may not be at all interested in the practical applications of his work, yet the further progress of industrial de-

velopment would eventually stagnate if basic scientific research were long neglected. . . .

Basic research leads to new knowledge. It provides scientific capital. It creates the fund from which the practical applications of knowledge must be drawn. . . .

[B]asic research is the pacemaker to technological progress.[13]

And, in another oft-quoted passage it cited a "perverse law" that "applied research invariably drives out the pure."[14]

In the 1950s and 1960s, these words would become the gospel of the scientific profession. For years, these passages would be repeated whenever examinations were made of the "health" of science — nearly always defined as whether basic university science was getting enough federal money. A typical sleight of hand was the transformation of the term basic research. Bush defined it as that "performed without thought of practical ends"; the more common, later, definition was that "which has no foreseeable use." The distinction is critical, for under Bush's definition, a scientist working on some fundamental problem may not worry about applications, but the person who funds the scientist should. Research "which has no foreseeable use" — like most of today's high-energy physics, astronomy, and some branches of mathematics — is impractical in the absolute sense. We call the latter "undirected" basic research and the former, i.e., research having some application — however long-range — in the mind of the sponsor, "purposive basic research."

The text of the Bush report and the appendices do *not* focus exclusively on basic research and the proposed foundation by any means. The report's main aim seems to have been to transmit the wartime leaders' sense of what had been necessary to pull off so many triumphs. Industrial uses of scientific research are underplayed because apparently the authors took it for granted that industry would seize on findings made in university and government laboratories; there is considerable discussion of tax and patent policies that form obstacles to the utilization of science — a cause Vannevar Bush would pursue thoughout his long career. A premise seems to be that colleges and universities exist to help industry; they need federal support in order to serve industry, and the public, better.[15] Even the phrase "basic research" is not used much: Bush more often employs the more meaningful phrase "the advance of science and its applications."

The Bush report places much emphasis on the advances in medical research and how effectively they were transferred into practice during the war. Enormous progress had been made in medicine between the wars, it says; penicillin, for example, saved many lives. Deaths from disease in the armed forces dropped from 14.1 to 0.6 per 1,000 from World War I to World War II. Dysentery had become a minor problem, and tetanus, typhoid, paratyphoid, cholera, and small pox were practically eliminated. During World War II, the United States' adoption of Fleming's observations about the penicillin mold and the extensive laboratory work at Oxford under Florey led to mass production of penicillin – the most conspicuous medical triumph of the war. But, the report cautions – as does the appendix dealing with medicine – comparable mechanisms do not exist in the civilian medical world to parlay these and future discoveries into better public health. A more uniform system of government-sponsored support of teaching and research is needed to assure this result.[16] So urgent was this need that the committee writing the appendix on medical research recommended a separate government foundation. Bush did not agree with this and recommended instead that his National Research Foundation sponsor medical, as well as military and other research.

The report is concerned with "the advance of science and its applications" in other areas: in the use of science to achieve full employment and create new industries, in encouraging the GIs then leaving military service to enter technical professions, in proposing a strong civilian role in military research, in recommending much more international exchange of scientific information. Indeed, by quoting part of the appendix dealing with education, Bush seemed to want the whole nation to learn science:

> [A] plan cannot be made which will select, and assist, only those young men and women who will give the top future leadership to science. To get top leadership there must be a relatively large base of high ability selected for development and then successive skimmings of the cream of ability at successive times and at higher levels. . . .

[W]e are not interested in setting up an elect. We think it much the best plan, in this constitutional Republic, that opportunity be held out to all kinds and conditions of men whereby they can better themselves. . . . We think it very important that every boy and girl shall know that, if he shows he has what it takes, the sky is the limit.[17]

Thus, the Bush report is not a paean to basic research. It is rather a broad-brush warning, by practical people who had managed a lot of difficult endeavors, that without a strong federal effort the new-found U.S. scientific leadership would be lost. The interconnectedness of basic science and its applications is implicit in these passages, quoted far less by the leaders of science in later years.

Science, by itself, provides no panacea for individual, social, and economic ills. It can be effective in the national welfare *only as a member of a team* [italics added]. . . .

There must be a stream of new scientific knowledge to turn the wheels of private and public enterprise. There must be plenty of men and women trained in science and technology for upon them depend the creation of new knowledge and its application to practical purposes.

More and better scientific research is essential to the achievement of our goal of full employment.

What we often forget are the millions of pay envelopes on a peacetime Saturday night which are filled because new products and new industries have provided jobs for countless Americans. Science made that possible, too.

New manufacturing industries can be started and many older industries greatly strengthened and expanded if we continue to study nature's laws and apply new knowledge to practical purposes.[18]

Finally, the models that Bush invokes for the proposed foundation, and for the other institutions envisaged to carry out the new policy, are not the old European universities, but the land-grant colleges noted above and the National Advisory Committee for Aeronautics (NACA), founded by the government in 1915 to "study the problems of flight with a view to their practical solution." The NACA had done much to improve U.S. aircraft performance in the period after World War I. Bush served as its chairman before moving to OSRD. Both the land-grant colleges and the NACA were concerned not with the creation of pure, new knowledge but with the transmission of knowledge and its application.

The argument we will make in following chapters leads to two conclusions. First, U.S. science should be reorganized to give equal weight to undirected basic research, purposive basic research, applied science, engineering, and technology. Instead of invoking undirected basic research as the central jewel in the research system's crown, we should stress the unique value of each separate jewel and their essential interdependence. This would redress the imbalance and force policymakers to devise better mechanisms for the transfer of basic knowledge to applications and vice versa. The change could reinvigorate basic research, too. We will describe how M.I.T., Bell Laboratories, and IBM, which do some of the best basic science in the country (and in the 1970s had fewer problems than many other research institutions), have done well because they make a point of intermingling basic and applied science.[19]

Second, there should be a change in the values of our scientists, particularly young people starting their careers, to stress the *interconnections* among disciplines, institutions, and across artificial barriers and obstacles now separating basic and applied science, engineering, and technology. In our interviews, senior research and development administrators often said these distinctions are artificial and restrictive. Why not let scientists build a system in which they can move back and forth between basic science and applications — as Townes was doing when he invented the maser? Why not let the cast of the show work fluidly together on the stage?

We need to replace the science profession's mistaken idea (found in the Bush report but misreading it) that science and its applications are a single tree whose roots are undirected basic research (Figure 2). Water the tree at its roots, and the fruits of technology will grow, automatically they seem to say. This may have appeared to be true in the early days when industry could exploit knowledge coming out of universities, when the government's national laboratories were young and dynamic, when there were corporate profits (!) which were being poured back into research, and when foreign competition was weak or nonexistent.

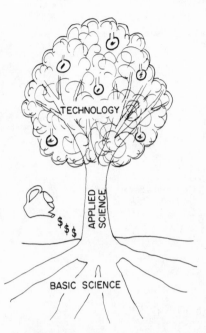

Figure 2 The conventional wisdom about the relationship between science and technology is represented as a single tree. If its roots, which are basic science, are watered, then the fruits, which are technology, will grow automatically. This widespread belief is disproved by the postwar experience of Great Britain (which has watered its basic science roots but has difficulty growing technology) and Japan (which has little basic science but grows technological fruits).

We believe the one-tree metaphor is incorrect. Great Britain's tree produces proportionately more Nobel Prize winners than ours, but its technology is wilting. Japan currently has only four Nobel Prize winners in science, but its tree's fruits are remarkable. Figure 3 proposes another metaphor, two separate but linked trees. A technology tree has its roots in capital and trained personnel and a trunk of applied science. Basic science is thought of as a separate tree, with a hydrologic system of its own. And the connection between the two . . . well, let's call them bees or bugs that cross-pollinate. (Indeed, the fact that Japanese technologists use the ideas of U.S.

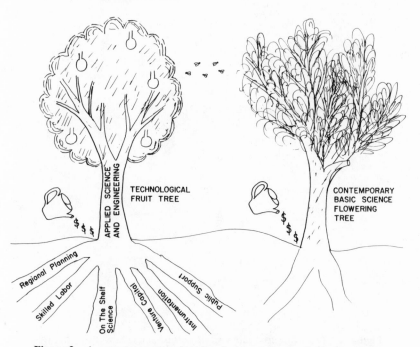

Figure 3   A more accurate metaphor is two trees, one for basic science and one for technology. This recognizes their distinct intrinsic character and the fact that they are nurtured separately by separate policies. Each tree, properly nourished, produces its own fruit: the basic science tree grows Nobel Prizes, and the more complex applied science-engineering-and-technology tree grows technology. Since the trees depend on each other as well, through bees that cross-fertilize, this model emphasizes the importance of establishing policies that nurture not only the technology tree in its own right, but the linkages between the two.

basic science so well illustrates another point made by our metaphor: the basic science tree can grow quite some distance away from the technologists who use it!)

It is increasingly clear that a more synergistic model of the interrelationship of science, engineering, and technology is not only more accurate historically, but more useful in policy design. Anna J. Harrison, a distinguished chemist who served as President of the American Association for the Advancement of Science, said in a recent, widely noted presidential lecture[20]:

> To me, there are common elements and interconnections within science, engineering, and technology that are attractive and compelling. . . . It is true that science drives engineering and technological innovation, but it is equally true that both engineering and technology drive science. The three processes, science, engineering, and technological innovation are synergistic. Each is dependent upon the other two; each supports the other two. It is this synergism that so enhances the total capabilities of science, engineering, and technology.

We would like professional scientists to ask themselves what they think they are discovering. What is the content of science? Is it one more bit of data wrested from Nature? Do all data have equal value, or do some data have more value than others? Do all studies approved by peer reviewers go forward? If we accept that value judgments can be made about the relative worth of different scientific findings, then we must establish standards and cannot pretend that no one, or some abstraction called a peer review system, runs science.

Our view is that science is and must be normative, even though many scientists try to deny it. A fable of Karl Popper, the well-known philosopher of science, illustrates our point. As quoted by Jacob Bronowski, it goes thus: Suppose a man wished to devote his life to science. Every day, for forty years, he writes down everything he observes in a notebook. He fills one notebook after another, recording the humidity, the latest racing results, the level of cosmic radiation, the stock market. When he dies, he leaves the notebooks to the Royal Society, which neither thanks him nor bothers to open the books. Without looking, the Society knows that they contain only a jumble of meaningless items.[21]

One answer to the question "What is science?" was offered by Ernst U. von Weizsäcker, former President of the University of Kassel in West Germany and the son of the famous German physicist. Von Weizsäcker suggested that the English word "truth" does not explain the goal of scientific discovery well at all. He suggested that of the two German words for truth, *Wahrheit* and *Wirklichkeit*, the latter conveys better the truth science seeks. *Wahrheit* means "truth" as opposed to falsehood. But science does not seek any old experimental result that is not false; it seeks *Wirklichkeit*, which means literally "the state of being work" and is usually translated as "reality." Its root is in a transitive verb that means to cause, to bring about, or to have an effect. *Wirken* also means "to weave" and this, von Weizsäcker said, is the true spirit of science. Bush may have thought so, too, for his report weaves science and all its useful applications so closely together that they appear to be one fabric.

But the followers of Bush pulled off a big switch. Those who came after and set up the system overemphasized the protection of basic science. Alan T. Waterman, the first Director of the National Science Foundation, who ran it from its founding in 1951 until 1963, epitomized this view. In a 1957 report to the President he wrote[22]:

> [B]asic research has certain characteristics which help . . . distinguish it from other forms of scientific activity. The search is systematic, but without direction save that which the investigator himself gives it to meet the challenge of the unknown. He is strictly on his own, guided primarily by his interest in learning more about the workings of nature.

Yet, interestingly, in the preceding paragraphs he gives science — by implication basic research — the credit for the rise of the United States!

> Science has played an important role in the rise of the United States from frontier land to world power. Indeed, the growth of our scientific effort parallels the growth of our strength as a Nation. The physical means to conquer wilderness, control natural forces, increase the length and, hopefully, the enjoyment of life, achieve national security — these things have come largely from ideas which observation, measurement, and other laboratory arts have developed into useful methods and machines at home and abroad.

Waterman considered the practical value of basic research so obvious that it was unnecessary to bore Congress by repeating it.

Not long ago it was considered necessary to justify basic research

which usually meant long and detailed accounts of its practical values
[italics added]. . . . Specific examples were cited frequently, maybe
too frequently, for some Congressmen's taste. . . . There is some
danger in overstating even the strongest case.

Waterman and the other followers of Bush succeeded too well. They
convinced Congress, the public, educators, and business leaders
that basic research should be set off with its own protected keep,
moat, army of defenders, and budget. But what they were really
doing was wittily summarized by "Engine Charlie" Wilson, an early
Secretary of Defense, who is supposed to have said: "Basic research
is when you don't know what you're doing."

The physicist at a mid-ranked university who applies to the
Department of Energy to do coal liquefaction research should not
have to dress up his proposal and resulting papers as undirected
basic research to win acceptance. It is not fair to the problem of
coal liquefaction (which is of national importance, after all), and
it hurts the integrity of basic research. Such a project might be,
in our terminology, either applied science or purposive basic
research — and should be judged by how well it will help to solve
the problem of coal liquefaction. Much that is called basic research
today is not cutting-edge basic science in the best sense of both
Bush's and Waterman's definitions. Further, despite the enormous
size of the whole research system (a structural problem, to be discussed later), real cutting-edge science is done at a small number
of institutions having very high quality people, a critical mass of
related research, and state-of-the-art instrumentation.

Outstanding basic research usually relies on a certain environment, on new instrumentation, and on discoveries in related fields.
This helps explain why "critical mass" institutions in Great Britain
and the United States have been so fruitful, and why many institutions are so often barren. Much of the flowering of knowledge
in the 1950s and 1960s may have come from cross-links between
quantum mechanics, solid state physics, and electrical engineering, from the growth of biological chemistry as a hybrid field, and
from the application of quantum mechanics and crystal structure
analysis to medical chemistry. Earlier, mathematics helped to
produce genetic theory, which produced hybrid corn and other
agricultural wonders. Likewise, scientific advance has come about

as a result of new technology: the computer has changed mathematical science, chemistry, and even aspects of biology. Taken in and of itself, a scientific discovery — such as Fleming's notice of the penicillin mold, or Sir George Cayley's theory of powered flight — may go unused for years until a better mix of need and entrepreneurship seizes it.[23] Price calls discoveries in this dormant stage "almost technologies." More recently, the basic technique for creating monoclonal antibodies was discovered in Britain's prestigious Laboratory of Molecular Biology at Cambridge University. But it was not thought to be useful enough to be patented. It was picked up promptly in the United States, and monoclonal antibody products are already proving powerful diagnostic tools, revolutionizing parts of medical care. The current U.S. success in biotechnology is partly the result of a rich mix of pure science, biomedical researchers eager to apply it, and the ease with which small firms can form to work on applications. Finally, the work itself is cross-disciplinary; it is engineering as much as biology. U.S. biotechnology, then, illustrates the kind of synergistic environment best for science *and* application.

III

Isn't this just history? Why be concerned in 1985 with what someone named Bush wrote back in 1945? What does it matter if scientists do "basic" or "applied" research, so long as they go on winning Nobel Prizes? Don't our achievements in science — our drastically improved understanding of disease, the electronics revolution, pharmaceuticals, biotechnology — speak for themselves? Why question the structure and values of a profession that has been so much more creative than its counterparts in other nations or than the science of the past?

The answer is that U.S. science could be more creative, in both basic science and applications. And it will have to be in the years ahead: 1985 is but a foretaste of 1995 or 2000. Our high-tech economy will be depending on our science for a continual stream of new ideas and new knowledge; foreign competition in science-based technology will be intense. It may come to a point at which scientific knowledge itself — the insight in the laboratory — *is* economic value, the thing which gives the product its principal worth, more than packaging or marketing (more on this later). Across all fields — not just the glamorous ones of molecular genetics and electronics, but also the less fashionable ones such as metallurgy, inorganic chemistry, mineralogy, low-energy physics, and zoology, to name a few — U.S. science will have to be highly productive, of both basic and applied knowledge. And the profession will have to engage in the effort to make the transition to applications that is vital to new technology and that we see vividly in the history of the atom bomb, the laser, the polio vaccine, and many other innovations.

So we write from concern for the 548,300 scientists and engineers now in universities, the 1,872,900 employed in business and industry, the 269,000 employed by the federal government, and the remaining 443,900 at work elsewhere who will determine whether our science enterprise is as productive as it can be.[24] They will make it happen — or hinder it from happening.

For it is they who decide which research to undertake, whether to direct their work along basic lines or turn to the applied aspect, or both. It is they who ratify or object to their university department's agreement with a company to proceed with a partnership arrangement. They, along with their grants administrators and institutional officers, create the atmosphere that surrounds a laboratory or research team and determines its expectations, goals, and morale. This pluralism, this democracy, is one of the great strengths of U.S. science and one reason it has been, in the narrow sense, successful. And it is a feature we dearly wish to preserve. Therefore, it matters what the members of the profession think; what their daily experiences are, what they believe in, and whether they despair.

This essay is aimed at the *profession* of science, a term we use to mean the professions of science and engineering, although the particular problems of engineering as distinct from science are treated too little here.

First, we discuss the growth of the postwar science institutions that came about thanks to the salesmanship of Bush and others after 1945. We will discuss how, nonetheless, the followers of Bush embedded another attitude, a basic-research-is-best mindset, in the structure and values of the postwar system — though not in every area. We note that the lobby for federal funding succeeded beyond its expectations. Over the years, federal support for science rose in universities and national laboratories too. In universities, it displaced the support from industry that had been common in the prewar era.

We will see how the belief in the separateness of basic science and applications became cant, and, to the profession's discredit, infected industry. Many U.S. companies in the 1960s and before — including the auto and steel giants — built gleaming new research laboratories that aimed to mirror the university laboratories. But management subscribed to the myth that science is something separate and lofty, requiring an incubation period of 30 years from discovery to product; i.e., they shared in the basic-research-is-best mindset. So they let their gleaming laboratories go their own way and rarely made use of their findings. What mattered, they thought, were the quarterly profit and loss statements. And when times got tough in the 1970s, they cut back much long-term applied work and closed down basic research to hunker down for what remains for too many a long winter of discontent. Belatedly, now that Japan is showing us how to seize on research findings (mostly ours) and catalyze them into fine-quality, low-price goods, U.S. business may be rediscovering — or rather discovering for the first time — the true importance of science. (Figure 4 illustrates the aggressive research and development activities of our major rivals and our own mixed record.)

Since our concern is with the productivity of the science profession, we will discuss how it has become confused by procedural mazes, administrative burdens, government regulation, and needless floundering for each tiny grant through a morass of rituals, among them peer review. These problems also stem from another myth — a corollary to the first one — that basic science can run itself, without judgments, without systematic thinking about where these myriad threads of knowledge lead. An alternative would be to keep science run from below, but have strong managers, who champion the work to the outside, establish linkages, and fend off government accountants. Such a system might free up scientists to carry out their work and public service activities, and might raise productivity and morale.

Finally, we will look at things the profession has *not* done, but should consider undertaking to meet the challenges ahead.

First, the profession ought to help narrow the gulf that separates the rapidly advancing frontier of scientific knowledge from the average citizen's understanding. We will need better technicians to operate our equipment — the Three Mile Island nuclear disaster should convince us of that. Businessmen will need to understand the scientific qualities of the products they produce and the products they compete against. Workers in a transformed workplace will have to be more skilled and understanding and able to adjust to new processes. For the past 30 years — with a brief exception after Sputnik — scientists' educational interest has centered almost exclusively on training the next crop of graduate students, i.e., their own replacements. This is an important goal, but hardly the only worthy one.

Second, U.S. science should become more international as foreign research improves and as big facilities become too expensive for any one nation to afford to build and run alone. Science's intrinsic internationalism is one of its most important qualities, but to nurture it in the midst of bustling international high-tech trade rivalry will be very difficult. The U.S. science profession is handicapped further by the isolationist tendencies of many, though not all, of its members. To overcome this, scientists will have to make an extra effort to travel and work abroad.

As science becomes more directly useful to commercial technology, it will probably be of greater military importance as well. U.S. science will see more attempts to inhibit academic freedom in the name of national security that characterized the Reagan administration from 1980 to 1984. There will be continued efforts to deter Eastern European and Soviet scientists from visiting our universities, more censorship of scientific findings before publication, and more attempts to prevent scientists from openly talking about certain basic research matters that the authorities consider sensitive. The profession will need to make sophisticated judgments about when academic freedom is compromised and stand up to government agencies (even agencies that are generous with research funds!) in this brave new world.

In all of this, we stress our interest in basic research and the fact that some research *has* no application — like astronomy, or much of pure mathematics, or some other fields. It is an advanced

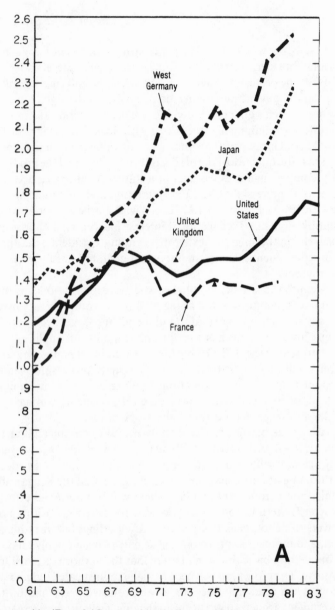

Figures 4A, 4B, and 4C Another challenge with important implications for U.S. technology and for international science is the increasing research effort of other nations relative to that of the United States.

Figure 4A The ratio of civilian research and development spending relative to gross national product of selected nations and the United

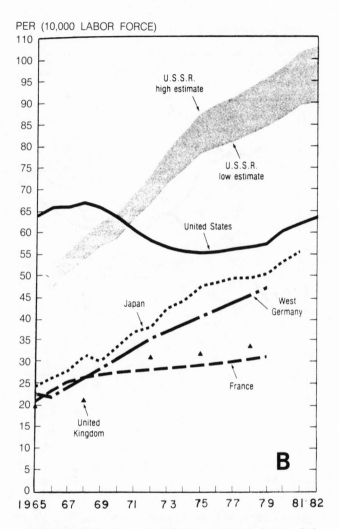

PER (10,000 LABOR FORCE)

States, 1961–1983. This shows the U.S. share to be *declining* relative to the others. (SOURCE: *Science Indicators 1982*, National Science Board, 1983, Figure 1-5, p. 8.)

Figure 4B   The "scientific intensity" of different nations' workforces, including that of the United States. This is the number of scientists and engineers engaged in research and development per 10,000 labor force population, 1965–1982. This shows that for many years the scientific intensity of the U.S. workforce *declined* relative to other countries. Now it is increasing, but likely to be overtaken by Japan and West Germany. A key point is that this portion of Japan's and West Germany's labor force (and most of the labor force of France as well) is engaged in work

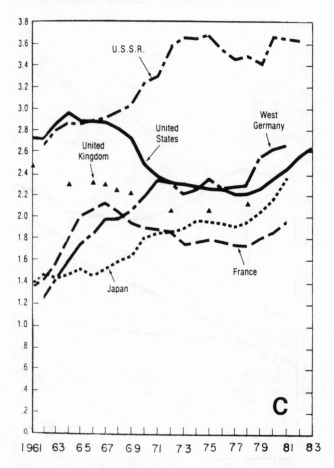

in the civilian sector, whereas approximately 50 percent of all U.S. scientists and engineers work on military-related projects (SOURCE: *Science Indicators 1982*, Figure 1-2, p. 5.)

Figure 4C   The U.S. position looks better when *all* research and development, including military, is compared with that of selected other countries. This shows the percentage of gross national product going to all research and development, military and civilian, 1961–1983. (SOURCE: *Science Indicators 1982*, Figure 1-4, p. 7.)

nation's duty to sponsor this kind of human inquiry on behalf of the species and to fund it as overhead. This is better than dishonest claims that this kind of science will fix the trade deficit. Therefore, the funding and structure of all science—undirected basic research, purposive basic research, and applied science (not to mention federal civilian development programs, which are another aspect of applications)—need to be reexamined and reformed, perhaps with a greater concentration of the very finest basic efforts in fewer places and the vast majority of effort dedicated to applied science. Fortunately, the White House had set up a new panel, headed by David Packard, to study structure and funding arrangements for science.

Wait, some of our scientist readers may be thinking. Maybe this so-called experiment in science criticism is a trap. Maybe it is but a fancy wind-up to a pitch to cut the federal basic research budget. The U.S. science community watches this particular indicator with an intensity that approaches fanaticism, all out of proportion to the small sum involved. The federal government spent an estimated $7.02 billion on basic research in 1983, which was 8.1 percent of the total R&D national investment of $86.5 billion.[25] Another $2.5 billion was spent on basic research that year by industry and non-profit organizations and universities, but the community pays less heed to that number, which we think is the more critical one. (The community is always fretting about federal funds for basic research and voicing "concern" for its "health"—a gripe that makes basic research sound like someone's sick old aunt, hardly flattering for an enterprise that is supposed to be the throbbing heart of our technological society!)

But to those readers we say now, up front in our essay, that we will not recommend a cut in basic research funding. Nor will we recommend a doubling of it either. Nobody knows, we argue, how big the basic research effort *should* be. And unless the sums are truly paltry, as they have been in Great Britain for too long, money is not the issue. The profession's structure and values are. The profession's fixation with marginal changes in the federal science budget decided in Washington reflects an unhealthy, morbid lack of initiative. It reflects an attitude that science lives by handouts and cannot put its own house in order and set its own priorities. Besides, with the growing role of states in setting local industrial

The current science policy debate misses the point by concentrating on improving budget prospects at the margins of established fields. Meanwhile, underlying problems are ignored. (SOURCE: V. V. Nalimov, *Faces of Science*, ISI Press, 1981, p. 20. Hereafter cited as Nalimov.)

policy, the profession should start looking to local government as much as Washington for "indicators" of how healthy or sick it is. Regionalism is another theme of our proposals for a restructured, re-valued U.S. science.

IV

Vannevar Bush was, at heart, a tinkerer and inventor. After he joined the M.I.T. faculty in 1919, he made his most important inventions: the network analyzer and the differential analyzer, which could solve differential questions having up to eighteen independent variables. Because the differential analyzer led to the first computers, Bush was one of the grandfathers of the computer revolution. A remarkable essay he wrote in the *Atlantic Monthly* in 1945 called "As We May Think" described the "memex," a small calculating and storage machine of the future; the article reads like a prescient description of today's home computer.

During World War I, Bush worked with a small company that invented a device for detecting German U-boats. Bush's frustration in trying to get the Navy to test it during the war led him to strongly favor civilian–military cooperation in areas of new technology and influenced his management of OSRD during World War II.

He tinkered with engines all his life, ever since his first Stanley Steamer broke down north of Boston, and he faulted the auto industry for its lack of inventiveness ("To be blunt, I think the men who manage the automotive industry are dumb," he wrote in 1970).[26] And on 6 August 1945, when the blast at Hiroshima revealed the existence of atomic weapons to the world, and the *New York Times* sought out Bush on Cape Cod, the mastermind of wartime science showed off his inventions for fog-clearing and flower-watering!

He also built a distinguished record of service, public and private. In addition to running the NACA and the OSRD, he served as president of the Carnegie Institution of Washington from 1939 to 1955 and after 1939 as a life member of the M.I.T. Corporation and its chairman from 1957 to 1959. He served as chairman of the board of Merck Pharmaceuticals from 1957 to 1962 ("My best times at Merck were in the research laboratories," he wrote later). He was proud of the fact that all five of the small firms he helped found had survived; one of them became Raytheon Corporation. A disservice for which he is remembered is a prediction he made that there never could be such a thing as an intercontinental ballistic missile; he was proved wrong soon after by the very inventiveness of U.S. military technology he had done so much to nurture.

In our essay, Bush, the engineer, epitomizes the dedication to broad ideals that we think should characterize the profession of science. We saw it in *Science—The Endless Frontier*. It is not surprising that he retained this vision even as the postwar profession became narrow. In Bush's later writings we found no trace of the basic-research-is-best arrogance characteristic of so many others on the postwar science scene. Indeed, Bush seemed concerned that professions not get too narrow. He admonished medical students not to forget their undergraduate liberal arts studies. He wrote that the business schools were teaching abstruse methodologies and omitting the rudiments. And he would return to the theme of a profession serving as a "ministry" to the public. In "The Art of Management," he wrote:

> The profession is a part of the society in which it acts. Its members expect, and intend to obtain, a proper share of the world's goods, in order that they may act effectively. But they are far more interested in other things than to join a mad scramble after riches. Their object in life is to minister to needs and welfare of those about them, by reason of special knowledge and special skills. . . .
>
> If a man's life is devoted to ministering to the people in this sense, and if his reward is the respect of the best of his peers, then he is a professional man. And, as such, he is the cement which has held society together since it first began.[27]

We will set Vannevar Bush aside for a while and instead talk about how his broader vision was betrayed by those who benefited from the case he built for science. We will talk about how postwar U.S. science, built on the shoulders of those who came after Bush, has deep inner problems, despite its outward show of success. These problems could hurt the country. The active help of U.S. scientists, in ways that are uncomfortable for them, is needed to turn this state of affairs around.

NOTES

[1] *Science—The Endless Frontier.* A report to the President on a Program for Postwar Scientific Research by Vannevar Bush, July 1945. Reprinted, July 1960, National Science Foundation, NSF 60-40. Hereafter referred to as Bush, *Science—The Endless Frontier.* This is the edition referred to throughout.

An interesting discussion of what "frontier" Roosevelt had in mind in his letter of request to Bush occurs in J. Merton England, *A Patron for Pure Science: The National Science Foundation's Formative Years, 1945-57*, National Science Foundation, Washington, D.C. NSF 82-24, pp. 107-108.

[2] Vannevar Bush, *Pieces of the Action* (New York: William Morrow, 1970), p. 64.

[3] Gerald Holton, "Science Technology and the Fourth Discontinuity," Proceedings and Conference on "Psychology and Society Information Technology in the 1980's" (Houston, Texas: 1982).

[4] Kenneth J. Bertrand, *Americans in Antarctica 1775-1948*, American Geographical Society Special Publication No. 39, pp. 198-201.

[5] *Encyclopedia Britannica*, 15th Edition, 1982, "Hatch Acts," — "Land Grant Colleges and Universities."

[6] Nathan Rosenberg, *Technology and Human Growth* (New York: Harper and Row, 1972), pp. 127-130.

[7] Daniel J. Kevles, *The Physicists, The History of a Scientific Community in Modern America* (New York: Alfred A. Knopf, 1978).

[8] Derek deSolla Price, "Sealing Wax and String: a philosophy of the experimenter's craft and its role in the genesis of high technology," Sarton Lecture, American Association for the Advancement of Science, May 1983, pp. 4, 5, 10-13, 16 *passim*, 22. Also William Broad, "Does Genius or Technology Rule Science?" *New York Times* (7 August 1984), pp. C1, C10.

[9] Nuel Pharr Davis, *Lawrence & Oppenheimer* (New York: Simon & Schuster, 1968), pp. 160-242 *passim*.

[10] See *Encyclopedia Britannica*, 1973 edition, article on Radar, pp. 995-997, vol. 18. C. P. Snow used the story of radar during the war as the paradigm of science in government, as illustrated in battle between Sir Henry Tizard and F. A. Lindemann, later Lord Cherwell, in *Science and Government*, Harvard University Press, 1961.

[11] Stephen Brunauer, "Einstein in the U.S. Navy," *Journal of the Washington Academy of Sciences*, 69:3 (1979), pp. 108-113.

[12] Bush, *Science—The Endless Frontier*, pp. 11, 22.

[13] *Ibid.*, pp. 18, 19, 22.

[14] *Ibid.*, p. 25.

[15] *Ibid.*, for example, pp. 21-22.

[16] *Ibid.*, pp. 13-16, 35, 64-69.

[17] *Ibid.*, pp. 24-25.

[18] *Ibid.*, pp. 11, 18, 10.

[19] See, for example, Paul E. Gray, "M.I.T. and Industry: A Partner-

ship," in *The Decades Ahead, an M.I.T. Perspective*, Proceedings of a symposium for senior executives, 24–26 June 1980, Industrial Liaison Program of M.I.T., p. 127H.

[20] Anna J. Harrison, "Common Elements and Interconnections," *Science*, 224 (1 June 1984), pp. 939, 940.

[21] J. Bronowski, *Science and Human Values* (New York: Harper, 1956), pp. 24 and 25.

[22] Alan T. Waterman, *Basic Research—A National Resource* (Washington, D.C.: National Science Foundation, 1957), pp. 1, 5, 6, and 7.

[23] Joshua Lerner, "The Discovery of Penicillin," unpublished paper, author's files.

[24] *Science Indicators 1982* (Washington, D.C.: National Science Board, 1983), Appendix Table 3-10, p. 258.

[25] *Ibid.*, pp. 236, 239.

[26] Vannevar Bush, *Pieces of the Action* (New York: Morrow, 1970), pp. 211, 212, 70–76; *Science is Not Enough* (New York: Morrow, 1967), pp. 211, 212.

[27] *Ibid., Science is Not Enough*, p. 69.

2

The Institutional Factor

W E HAVE DESCRIBED the basic-research-is-best mindset that came to dominate the culture and values of U.S. science after World War II. This chapter explores how this attitude shaped the nation's science institutions in the postwar period and some of the consequences. One way is that a whole generation of scientists has grown up in this system, feeling entitled to receive federal funds in the name of eventually producing applications, but with the real aim of doing basic research to win status according to the profession's increasingly narrow standard. This institutional factor now hinders efforts to couple science to the nation's economic and technological needs.

Much must be done by the way of institutional reform to make U.S. science as productive as possible of both basic knowledge and applications in the years ahead, but institutions are hard to change. One might whimsically compare them to ballistic missiles: once launched they follow their own trajectories; you cannot recall them; finally, it takes a veritable storm to make them change course.

This chapter will trace the growth of the institutional factor and the problems it has created. We argue that current institutional structure and management arrangements impede close links between science and applications. Moreover, the myth of the

divorce between basic science and applications hurts both. Individual scientists feel they are fulfilling their profession's highest
goals only when they are doing basic research and feel it is proper
to ignore whether their work is contributing to some overall applications scheme.

Meanwhile, applied science policy is, quite simply, a mess. The
federal government starts and stops applied science and development programs with frenetic speed, with changes in administration, changes at the assistant secretary level, changes in the heads
of federal bureaus, or to appease powerful interest groups lobbying through Congress. As a result, while the amount of applied
science done in universities is increasing (mainly due to recent federal defense budget increases), much of it is totally fragmented
and uncoordinated.

But the profession shrugs off this chronic instability in applied
science with the old cant. What does it matter, so long as money
keeps flowing for basic research? Isn't basic research "scientific
capital," the fount from which technology flows, the wellspring
for innovation? All too often, the process by which science becomes technology does not concern today's scientists. And the
fact that the incubation period between science and innovation
has been set by scholars at 30 years (conveniently longer than the
remainder of their careers) relieves them of responsibility, they
think, to see that applications come forth. For all they care, the
process of innovation might as well be magic. This insouciance is
reflected in federal science policy, whose arrangements for civilian
applied science and development are woefully inadequate. This
basic-research-is-best mentality robs the applied sector of the
best brains, care for integrity of the enterprise, and policy attention. Moreover, the administration of basic research is characterized by a weak management style that permeates the applied side
as well and permits applied projects to be politicized, turned off,
turned on, turned to the left, turned to the right, broken up, and
to yield, in the end, only scraps.

This chapter will also discuss the peculiar science policies of
the Reagan administration. In many ways the President's science
adviser, George A. Keyworth II, epitomizes the basic-research-is-
best mindset that we find so insidious. And Keyworth has backed

boosterish words with deeds, providing some of the most generous funds for basic science of any science adviser in the past decade—while in effect announcing that more money for basic research will fix the U.S. economy. Meanwhile, he has hacked away at applied projects, demonstration programs, and the federal civilian applied science infrastructure that we argue is invaluable to the orderly transformation of pure knowledge into economic value. Keyworth's maverick views on defense, such as his support for futuristic "Star Wars" antiballistic missile systems, rightly fill many in the science community with doubt. But on the plus side he has also been more willing to experiment with the institutional structure, a gameness we feel is long overdue. However, the story starts back in 1946.

I

Bush's report to President Roosevelt, *Science—The Endless Frontier*, argued for a single independent foundation run by a board of nine qualified citizens. The foundation would sponsor research in the physical sciences, in medicine, and in military matters; it would analyze national policy on research and science education. A separate science advisory board was proposed to evaluate and integrate all technical research sponsored by other government departments. It was a sweeping order which was never carried out.

Neither President Truman nor some in Congress liked Bush's proposal to give a group of nine citizens control over funds outside of normal government channels. They also objected to Bush's plan to have rights to inventions derived from government-sponsored research rest with the individual inventor. Truman vetoed the first version of the bill creating the new foundation.

In the end, the final mandate of the foundation in law differed from Bush's original plan. Besides a powerful board to run the foundation and make policy, the law provided for a presidentially appointed director with whom the board would share authority. Bush had proposed a division of national defense and a division of medical research, but by the time the bill passed, neither was included. The scope of the foundation was also narrowed. Bush had wanted it to "develop and promote a national policy for scientific research and scientific education," but the act limited this authority to basic research and science education.[1]

Nonetheless, the Director and the National Science Board were given a national policy role. They were to "appraise the impact of research upon industrial development and upon the general welfare," and "evaluate scientific projects undertaken by agencies of the Federal Government."

Although the mandate of the National Science Foundation (NSF) retained some of the broad, ambitious themes Bush wanted, the early leaders of NSF and early members of the National Science Board would consciously decide to play a more limited role. They would decline to have the Navy's research program moved under their jurisdiction; they sidestepped opportunities to review other federal programs. When conflicts appeared with more powerful agencies, they demurred, saying that the foundation was only in the business of supporting basic research.

The early debates about the foundation's role are still relevant today. Was it to support only elite institutions? Or should it, as the politically potent land-grant colleges urged, distribute its money geographically to develop top-quality institutions where there had been none? As other research agencies sprang up in other government departments, Bush argued that the need for the Foundation's coordinating role was stronger than ever.

> The recipients of these grants are quite happy, they have several sources of funds and can trade about, but they are likely to become adept at that sort of political maneuvering at the sacrifice of more virile characteristics.[2]

Which is exactly what happened. In time, the NSF avoided involvement in national policy and chose to fill in the cracks left by other agencies; it claimed a unique role only in supporting undirected basic research. Thus opened the first rift in what became a gulf between basic research and the rest of the enterprise.

The chances for central management of postwar science diminished for other reasons as well. In 1945–1946, the atomic scientists, who were now world-famous thanks to the bomb, were fighting ardently for civilian control of atomic energy. A crucial argument in their fight to make the Atomic Energy Commission (AEC) a civilian agency was that atomic research could produce not only bombs but also benefits for mankind, in agriculture, medicine, and industry. Civilian applications could emerge, they argued, only if this research was done in a civilian agency and if there were few barriers between civilian and military atomic research. They succeeded with the passage of the Atomic Energy Act in 1946; the AEC then became the major civilian sponsor of physics research.[3]

Other forceful personalities had plans too. Admiral Harold G. Bowen, a Rickover-type figure, was determined to set up a glamorous research arm in the Navy. Bowen was a forceful officer smarting, first, from his banishment to be head of the Naval Research Laboratory by the regular Navy bureaus, and second, from the way the Office of Scientific Research and Development (OSRD) had mistreated the Navy, in his view, during the war. Bowen and his team of officers toured the campuses of the elite universities and offered them generous terms to come under Navy patronage. They had $24 million in contracts by the time the law establishing the Office of Naval Research (ONR) was signed in August 1946. The sum was handsome: three out of every four dollars that the federal government spent on research were being spent by the ONR. Some in the scientific community and the Bureau of the Budget were concerned about this overwhelmingly military support of university science; later a transfer of much of ONR's program to the NSF was arranged — but never carried out.[4]

The ONR thus became a generous patron of university science and was well liked by those who received its largesse. The careers of many of today's scientific leaders were shaped by the perceptiveness and informality of the ONR. Scientists were poor then, and a few thousand dollars a year from an understanding ONR officer sometimes meant the opening up of a new research area or career path. Many of those we interviewed talked nostalgically about the old ONR as having been the only federal patron that had really understood how to mix the Navy's mission needs with a sharp eye for advancing high-quality basic science.

It was no surprise, then, that when the NSF was formed, the obvious candidate for director was ONR's chief scientist, Alan T. Waterman. It also followed that, when Congress nearly zeroed the fledgling NSF's first budget request, Waterman should have turned to his friends in the military and asked them to support NSF's cause in Congress. In return, Waterman promised he would not poach on the military's research turf.

The same thing happened with medical research. Medicine had been supported on an emergency basis by the OSRD during the war. When OSRD's medical committee dissolved, it turned over forty-four research contracts to the National Institute of Health (NIH), founded in 1930. As the NIH grew in the late 1940s, institutes were added for mental health, dental science, neurological diseases, and microbiology. By 1951 the NSF faced a powerful rival in the NIH in sponsoring medical research. Waterman decided to confine the NSF's role, therefore, to the most basic aspects of biomedicine.[5]

Thus, by the time the NSF opened its doors in 1951, university scientists had fragmented into four overlapping constituencies: the medical researchers who looked mainly to the NIH, a distinguished group at the elite research universities sponsored by the ONR, the physicists sponsored by the AEC, and the group forming around Waterman at the NSF. In addition, the Army and the Air Force were building up their sponsorship of research. There were the older groups, such as the National Advisory Committee for Aeronautics, the U.S. Weather Bureau, and the U.S. Geological Survey, as well.

II

In our view, in the early 1950s when Waterman, the National Science Board, and the Bureau of the Budget made critical choices about the NSF and the growing federal–university science system, the seeds of our present troubles were sown. The tone and values of the system were set on a course that would lead them away from the main ideas in *Science — The Endless Frontier*.

The change was unwitting, and it seemed logical at the time. For example, much of Waterman's and the board's reluctance to play a more ambitious role was due to the problem they were having in justifying the agency's tiny program before its Congressional oversight committees. If their modest initial effort was under so much attack, they reasoned, more ambitious schemes would make matters worse. In addition, their enthusiasm for basic science reflected the general euphoria about science of the 1950s. But from today's vantage point, historic opportunities seem to have been lost.

First, unmanaged diversity replaced Bush's concept of a national science policy and central planning for science. The notion that a committee of nine wise heads could run the postwar science system as the OSRD had managed the wartime one died with the delay in creating the NSF and the emergence of more powerful research patrons in other agencies. Though the NSF was charged with evaluating all federal science efforts, Waterman and the National Science Board let this idea drop in 1954 with hardly a murmur. So much for the institutionalization of a national science policy.

Diversity and lack of central control were not seen as a problem, however, and when the scale of the endeavor was small, it didn't matter. First, the scientists were pleasantly surprised at the government's generosity and were eager to be patronized. The diffusion of government sponsors was justified on the grounds that a single sponsor for physics or biology might be prejudiced and unfairly bias the development of a field. But this reasoning, invoked then and now as an argument against strong research managers, overlooked a key distinction in the Bush report. Bush had advocated the board of nine wise heads to be central planners for science, to do what today's business jargon calls strategic planning. Neither Bush nor anyone else advocated centralized *execution* of the plan. Science thus evolved in an increasingly convenient, diverse — and headless — fashion. As Daniel S. Greenberg wrote of the postwar period, science was unexpectedly rich, but "it was also rudderless in its affluence."[6]

Second, growth became the system's dominant mode of successful operation and perhaps its only one. The system institutionalized Bush's recommendation that science requires a certain freedom and that scientists are best qualified to run their own affairs. And since every experiment would breed four new questions requiring answers, four new projects could be justified to follow on after every one. Thus, run from below, the system had no internal means of judging among the four follow-on projects, i.e., of setting priorities. This flaw remained hidden in the days of affluence. But because of it, the community to this day nearly tears itself apart when funds are tight. (Keyworth, in a promising recent move, has insisted that a few subfields such as planetary science set their own priorities for limited funds.)

Thus, the institutional management pattern tended to be passive, scientist-oriented, and discipline-oriented. These were values emphasized by Waterman during his long tenure as director from 1951 until 1963, as described by NSF historian J. Merton England:

> Convinced that science policy must come from the scientific community, not from Washington, he was really a spokesman for basic science and its protector in Washington, not an instrument serving the short-term goals of a political administration.

And as for the orientation of the NSF program managers, who made grants in biology, chemistry, physics, and so on:

> [T]hey were even more ardent advocates of support for basic science research in their disciplines. Science policy to a program director meant most of all more money for his field of science. Even if he were a permanent member of the staff rather than a rotator on a year's leave from a university, a research program director maintained close association with working scientists throughout the country and regarded them as his colleagues. . . .
>
> The professional staff emphasized high-quality science, that which the peer review system judged most worthy of support.[7]

This philosophy is a far cry from the Bush report, which emphasizes central planning by the board and a scientific community responding to national needs.

The NSF philosophy became the opposite: policy was deliberately left in the hands of the university scientists, mostly through peer review. Although in the early days there was so little money that only the elite institutions passed normal reviews, as the system became richer, it spread the money around and began trying to develop research excellence in institutions previously unable to compete. As one of the managers of the NSF earth sciences program in the 1950s recalled, the reviews immediately showed which proposals were best and which were worst, leaving a large middle group. If the middle group had proposals of equal merit from M.I.T. and from, say, Jonesboro Teachers College, "We gave it to Jonesboro College," he said.[8] The system thus encouraged more and more Jonesboros to aspire to play the basic research game and emulate the high science done at the top-ranked schools.

The growth in federal research funds going to colleges and universities was astonishing. The overall shifts it caused are shown in Figure 5. In 1960 universities and colleges performed an estimated $433 million in basic research coming from all sources. By

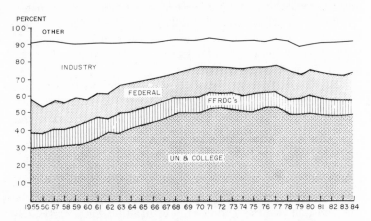

Figure 5 The salient change in the performance of basic research in the United States in the postwar period is the gradual withdrawal of U.S. industry, which performed approximately one-third in the 1950s and early 1960s. Colleges and universities, which performed 30 percent in 1955 (almost as much as industry), performed 50 percent by 1968 and 49 percent in 1984. Chapters 2 and 3 discuss the profound implications of this shift and of corresponding shifts in the performance of applied research for the national technological effort. (SOURCE: Chart adapted from Bruce L. R. Smith and Joseph J. Karlesky, *The State of Academic Science* (New York, Change Magazine Press, 1971), Vol. 1, p. 22, Fig. 4. Recent data from National Patterns of Science and Technology Resources, 1984, National Science Foundation, 1984, Table 8, p. 33.)

1982 that figure had grown in current dollars to $4.9 billion. In constant 1972 dollars the increase was from $622 million to $2.3 billion. When the federal applied research and development budget is added in, the figures are still higher. And development monies were easier to spread geographically. So a system that started as a way to continue modestly supporting fifteen to twenty established institutions became an odd hybrid, part political pork barrel and part peer-judged quality (and discipline-constrained) science. The case for nonstop growth was argued in a series of National Academy of Sciences (NAS) reports on specific disciplines, such as the Pake report on physics. These argued that current funding levels were not enough and that only lack of funds stood between the field's current accomplishments and future breakthroughs.

There was explosive growth in medical research. Federal support enabled the number of teaching hospitals, departments, faculty, and level of research funds to grow. Between 1950 and 1980, the number of medical schools grew from 72 to 112, or 55 percent. The number of M.D. degrees awarded rose in the same period, from 5,600 to 14,900.

This amazing growth reflected many profound shifts in the structure and funding of American medicine. Early in the century, the U.S. medical profession had recognized that the M.D. degree alone was insufficient to keep doctors abreast of new advances; it encouraged M.D.s to stay on for a residency before starting practice. Medical schools were assuming more research duties even before World War II. Then the Bush report and the medical science lobby spurred postwar interest in research-intensive, scientific medicine that gave the schools a powerful adjunct in the NIH. (By 1948 it had so many units added that it became the National Institutes of Health.)

Then came dramatic changes in health care financing in the 1960s: federal reimbursement for patient care under social security (not to mention veteran's care under the Veterans Administration system). These enabled doctor–researchers to offer very sophisticated care that was an adjunct to their research to virtually the entire patient population, at no extra cost to patients themselves. To borrow an analogy from the defense industry, suddenly there was a guaranteed customer for almost any technological advance in medicine. The doctors acquired, so to speak, captive buyers, a guaranteed market "pull."

The postwar growth of federal research patronage spurred different kinds of developments in medical research, some healthy, some not. For one thing, the discrepancy was particularly awkward between the justification for federal support and the researchers' professional desire to go off on their own and do basic research.

The "application" of biomedical research was politically very attractive, namely, that a cure would be found for some disease or that a particular organ of the body, researched massively by the federal government, would stop suffering, so to speak, all across the land. As members of Congress recognized the political appeal of starting new named, targeted NIH programs, their rapid growth became inevitable.

Of course, the medical scientists who benefited from this popularity could not promise that the chances of a cure would improve in direct proportion to the amounts of money voted by happy Congressmen. But they colluded with the politicians because it is true that basic research really does (synergistically, we might add) produce breakthroughs. Such basic research funds, they could argue, would be churlish to refuse. The outstanding case, of course, was President Nixon's "war on cancer" in which the political momentum for a large new program overwhelmed the scientists' doubts that a transfusion of government funds would cause a "breakthrough" anytime soon. All they could conclude was that inducing thousands more researchers into the field through a new program would not hurt, and might help, not only cancer but also other fields. So the scientists took the money and did their research. To the scientists' credit, they tried to reorganize Nixon's plan to ensure that it had more scientific integrity. But still today, the management of the program reflects its somewhat schizophrenic character, with the highest-level advisory board composed of luminaries, such as industrialist Armand Hammer, who reflect the political constituency for a "cure" and a subordinate scientific board that runs the operational aspect of the program.

Especially when it was smaller, the NIH exemplified what we argue are ideal conditions for extracting both applications and good basic science from a single organization: there was both pluralism and synergism, pressure from the top to find applications and enough high-quality science to attract the best people. Moreover, various of the NIH's directors have been strong managers, taking responsibility for the technical integrity of the whole and even, on occasion, saying no to politicians or powerful medical lobby groups. In this sense, the NIH system proves our thesis, as parts of it have been highly productive. But many in the biomedical community criticize a great deal of the NIH's work as pure basic-research-is-best for its own sake, and too narrow and self-centered and divorced from other research and from applications.

Perhaps the most instructive aspect of the biomedical research system from our point of view is the coupling of practical necessity and basic science embodied in the M.D.-Ph.D. system. After the war, more and more M.D.s were encouraged to get the Ph.D. as well. Thus, even while pursuing abstruse research careers, they would not forget their bedside experiences and responsibilities. The M.D.-Ph.D. corner of the overall biomedical research system is credited by many with having made biomedical science so productive of applications. It is one reason for concern about the possible decline in M.D.s who go on for the Ph.D. discussed in Chapter 4.

The political appeal of dollars for defense research is similar to that of dollars for biomedicine. In defense, there are eager politicians voting funds for research and a guaranteed customer in the armed services and intelligence agencies. But as with biomedicine, the result has been a mixed bag. On the one hand, those parts of the defense science community that are synergistic have made tremendous contributions linking basic knowledge to applications (we will see this synergism between defense science and industry in the electronics story in the next chapter). On the other hand, the defense establishment has sometimes been as weak on applications as parts of the NIH. Defense research agencies generally do a good job of moving ideas from the pure knowledge stage to what we would call purposive basic research, and along the spectrum to new hardware and a customer in the armed services. Moreover, it uses a management tool, namely, the classification of all projects under headings of 6.1, 6.2, 6.3, etc., depending on where they fall in the basic-to-applied spectrum, which helps to organize the transition to technology. Finally, under the influence of the university scientists it sponsors, the Department of Defense (DOD) has constructed critical mass centers of high science around the country (the AEC, similarly influenced by its university-based physicists, did likewise).

But DOD is criticized by many thoughtful people for having weak management of the transition to applications of "almost technologies," such as advanced rocket fuels or ceramic engines. This tends to happen with developments which there is as yet no specific customer lobbying for, yet where the underlying promise is clear. As on the civilian side, defense projects at this level often get started, stopped, and redirected arbitrarily, and the linkage with industry (with some stunning exceptions) is uncoordinated. So from World War II through 1970, defense research suffered from the same affliction: strong basic research and sometimes weak management of applications. Following congressional pressure, DOD cut off and transferred much of its basic research in the 1970s — and some people argue that a proper balance between the two has not been achieved in the DOD, even under the Reagan administration, which has poured funds into DOD *development* accounts but has been less generous with DOD *basic* research, as we shall see.

III

The template of this federal institutional pattern was printed on the universities, where the structure, funding, and values of research activity changed markedly after the Bush report and the sprouting of federal research agencies. Basic-research-is-best came to dominate the thinking of university people seeking funds, as well as research managers in government giving them out — even though, paradoxically, the amounts for applied research were sometimes greater and easier to spread around geographically.

Another impact of the basic-research-is-best attitude was to downgrade the role of science in industry, the roles of engineering and of invention. Generations of graduate students were taught that to work in industry had less status than to pursue basic academic research. Echoes of this are heard today as faculty members complain that today's graduate students are deserting academic science for industry. We will see in the next chapter how industrial research, which had enjoyed a coequal status with that done in universities, has been downgraded as the federal–university system has grown.

Even institutionally, engineering was given second-class status. While engineers in the United States have never had the low rank they have in Great Britain (a problem which shows up in Britain's difficulty in producing and marketing advanced technology), engineers in the United States nonetheless have less status than scientists. A symbol of this unfortunate relationship is the story of the National Academy of Engineering (NAE), which finally in 1982, as a result of a strong effort, became coequal with the NAS.

The NAS had been founded as a private organization with a federal charter in Abraham Lincoln's day in 1863. The principal scientists, such as Joseph Henry, represented our practical nineteenth-century tradition of applied science. But they also wanted to distinguish science from quackery and put it more on a footing with European high science. So the NAS evolved into an elite—which is what it was supposed to be, after all—but an elite which, by the mid-twentieth century, represented mainly the basic-research-is-best point of view.

This had consequences for the engineers, for they seemed permanently seated below the salt: they had no academy of their own nor did they, for the most part, qualify for membership in the NAS. But in 1964 they succeeded in having their own academy established.

However, this National Academy of Engineering was not founded as a separate organization with its own federal charter parallel to the NAS, but as a subordinate organization whose right to exist derived from the NAS charter. The NAE elected its own members, ran its own finances, and had its own program until the 1970s, when the program was merged with that of the NAS and they both became run through the NAS governing arm, the National Research Council (NRC). Management of NAS and NAE programs devolved on the governing board of the NRC. But representatives of the NAE were allowed fewer seats on the governing board than representatives of the NAS, so the NAS effectively controlled the NRC and its program. Finally in 1982, after a crisis in graduate engineering education and other issues had galvanized the engineers to lobby for recognition, the NAE won equal status on the board with the NAS. Nevertheless, engineering as a profession distinct from science had a long way to go in getting equal recognition from the general public.

Finally, the system discouraged any university from unifying disciplines. If a department of electrical engineering set out to compete with those at other universities in hiring the hottest graduate students and obtaining federal research grants, it was less likely to concern itself with the manufacturing firm just down the street. Once a department of oceanography set its sights on becoming a national "center of excellence" by Washington's standards, and by the standards of would-be "peers" in other centers around the country, it would become scornful of applied science relating to local fishing problems.

This narrowness is in contrast to the way many of the best U.S. universities traditionally functioned. Ironically, the institutions that maintained their industrial ties came through the 1970s the best — and are poised to remain strong in the future. Just before becoming President of M.I.T., Paul E. Gray gave a talk about the Institute's historic ties to industry. He noted that its 1861 charter says the Institute's purpose is to educate students in science *and its applications*; this set M.I.T. off from many other universities of the day. Elihu Thompson, whose electric company merged with Edison's to become General Electric, was both on the faculty and acting president of M.I.T. When William Lyman Underwood, whose grandfather had founded the country's oldest cannery, asked M.I.T. to study food spoilage, this led to the creation of M.I.T.'s Nutrition Department and to a revolution in the food industry. Even Vannevar Bush, who was M.I.T.'s Dean of Engineering in the 1930s and later the Chairman of the M.I.T. Corporation, tinkered with a little company in Medford that eventually became

Raytheon. These links, Gray said, gave "rise to powerful intellectual and technological relationships that have influenced the shape of M.I.T. and of American industry in profound ways."[9] Gray's story illustrates our point: M.I.T. maintained a strong philosophy of the importance of *linking* basic and applied science, of tying the university setting to real-world needs. Both M.I.T.'s basic science and the problems it has addressed have benefited. Unfortunately, most U.S. universities lacked such strong, indigenous philosophies. So, over 40 years, as federal support grew, they came to believe in the basic-research-is-best message that the system transmitted on all wavelengths.

IV

This was the institutional setting for U.S. research in 1945–1970 — which in retrospect was an aberrant period in U.S. history. At least through 1968, it was a period of unprecedented growth in the gross national product and of unprecedented U.S. hegemony in the world in military, economic, technological, and scientific terms. Characteristically, the academic research community lost no opportunity in implying that federal basic research funding was causing this prosperity. Now, none of these conditions holds, but the U.S. science system, its structure and values, have remained as unchanged as if we were still living in the 1960s.

Indeed, the system's problems were noted at the time. Looking back through the history, we found a fascinating series of justifications and warnings in a collection of essays about the value of research commissioned by the House Committee on Science and Astronautics in 1963. The Committee had asked, rightly, what level of federal funding, and balance among different sciences, was needed "to keep the United States . . . [in a] position of leadership *through* basic research *in the advancement of science and technology and their economic*, cultural and military applications" [italics added]. Most of the respondents conveniently reinterpreted the question to ask, what was needed for the U.S. to improve its basic research?

But a few authors, among them Hendrik Bode of Bell Labora-

*The postwar science establishment's paradigm: Basic Research marches valiantly into the future. (*SOURCE: Nalimov, p. 222.)*

tories, Edward Teller, Arthur Kantrowitz, and Alvin Weinberg, warned that the transfer of basic knowledge to applications was not getting enough attention. Kantrowitz argued that since universities do not invent things, they train graduate students to believe that fundamental discovery, not invention, is the highest goal of science. "This attitude presents an intolerable obstacle to the achievement of excellent university education in applied science," he wrote.[10]

"Most of the superior Ph.D.'s coming from our universities have a primary interest in basic rather than applied science," warned Bode[11]:

> [U]ntil comparatively recent years, science and technology have pursued essentially independent courses. . . . The deliberate application of science to technology is primarily a phenomenon of the war and post-war years. . . .
>
> [T]he deliberate application of science to technology . . . presents a number of problems . . . [T]hese difficulties and unevennesses in the transition from science to technology represent the most critical aspect of the issues raised by the questions of the House committee—the aspect that most needs attention if the country is to maximize the yield from its investment in basic science. . . .

Bode then suggested ways to maximize this yield—through government actions, special curricula, and training for applied scientists who "should be on the same footing as the typical pure scientist," and a general realization of "how much science and technology actually have in common." But the warnings in the volume were drowned out by the politically powerful champions of the basic-research-is-best school, who would be mortified to be "on the same footing" with engineers and applied scientists.

Structural flaws began appearing in the 1970s, when the decline in real dollars going to university research exposed the system's weaknesses. These problems can be expected to remain, despite recent budget increases, if the reform is not undertaken. Somewhat arbitrarily, we divide these flaws into three categories, although they make up a larger, less easily defined problem.

Weak management.   The present system emphasizes a model of science proceeding relentlessly, as the cliché goes, according to its own inexorable laws. This positivist–reductionist view of scientific progress is conveniently abstract, suggesting that no human intervention is needed at the managerial level. Peer review diffuses responsibility still more, since reviewers act anonymously and are not held responsible for their decisions. Indeed, they are shielded

by anonymity and guarantees of impunity however erroneous —
even outrageous — their reviews (we discuss peer review further in
Chapter 4). As we have seen, this enables judgments about science
to be made only at the level of the sub-subspecialties, provides no
mechanism for judgment calls among subfields, or setting priorities among disciplines.

Barry Bozeman and Dong Kim of Syracuse University published an attitudes survey of NSF program officials. Unwittingly,
it showed that Waterman's stamp persists. Analyzing survey ques-
tionnaires returned by 199 NSF officials, Bozeman and Kim
found that the older and better-salaried they were, the less they
were likely to believe that private industry was effective, or that
research should serve social objectives, and the more likely they
were to believe that basic research is an end in itself. Bozeman and
Kim concluded:

> Despite massive government science activity, there is strong
> resistance among many scientists and science policy-makers to
> planning or directing science. Perhaps more than in other indus-
> trial nations, the United States government's policy-making agen-
> cies for science have worked in partnership with (or have been co-
> opted, depending on one's view) by the nongovernmental scientific
> community.[12]

This passive view of management's role in science conflicts
sharply with the descriptions we received of how major, top quality science institutions are run. At Bell Laboratories, we were told,
basic research is not funded for its own sake. (Perhaps this is a
myth, passed along by university scientists who hope that Bell
Laboratories fits their favorite assumptions!) Although many
researchers there work on fundamental problems, they are
selected by managers who want their expertise. Federal science
managers (with exceptions, as we said) tend to believe they should
not play a comparable, driving role.

An unintended result of this management style is that scientists
have abdicated authority to the green-eyeshaders at the Bureau of
the Budget, now the Office of Management and Budget (OMB).
By default, OMB became a potent manager of science through the
mechanism of the annual federal budget cycles. If science were

setting its own priorities, and making its own long-term plans, the importance of yearly budgets would diminish, as would the scientists' obsession with marginal changes in them.

The OMB has had to force priorities upon U.S. science: sometimes it has forced specialties to pay more attention to national needs, and sometimes it has gutted fields that in its judgment have not been productive. OMB does this only because the scientific community has failed to do these things itself. We argue that while there is some need for stronger coordination at the top, particularly of government civilian applied science programs, also there should be stronger self-management by scientists. The government might stop nitpicking if only scientists showed themselves better able to set their priorities responsibly themselves. Only in this way will the community be able to avoid the fate Don K. Price once described in the title of a paper he wrote in *Daedalus*: "The Endless Frontier Is a Bureaucratic Morass."

Archaic university departments. The absence of strong management within the science system leaves it vulnerable to powerful institutional pressures that are far less worthy. OMB micromanagement is one; another is the ordinary university department, which remains administratively sacrosanct and thoroughly discipline-oriented. Its *raison d'être* seems often to be to milk the federal government for all the money it can get.

The seeds of their influence were sown in the 1950s, when the federal science agencies organized internally into sections of biology, physics, and so on, intended to correspond to traditional departments. These agencies did this to better serve their budding university clientele, but the result has been to reinforce artificial subdivisions of science and put funding officials and university departments in lockstep.

This may be good for science that happens to fall in the mainstream of a traditional field, but it is hard on work that pushes at the fringes. NSF historian England's remark about how much NSF grants administrators identified with their counterparts in university faculties indicates the social underpinnings of the arrangement which became common in other federal science agencies.

Yet it should be obvious that the explosion of knowledge that has occurred as a result of all this research (it is said that 90 percent of the scientists who ever lived are alive today) often blurred or upset traditional disciplinary boundaries. Disciplinary boundaries are but lines drawn in sand. Rich universities (or merely ingenious ones) have been able to set up new departments or institutes (especially in the 1960s, when money was available), to enable merging fields to come together, or to nurture promising offshoots.

The number of such research institutes on U.S. campuses grew explosively from 2,987 in 1965 to 5,024 in 1972, but stabilized at the level in 1975 as the financial crunch set in. These institutes are typically interdisciplinary and relate to national needs — the environment, transportation, and so on. Recent novel examples include the Whitehead Institute at M.I.T. incorporating relevant parts of the life sciences, physical sciences, engineering, and medicine, and the small astrophysics group at the Fermi National Accelerator Laboratory near Chicago.

The departments' power did not matter so much in the 1950s and 1960s, when there was more money for add-ons as new disciplines sprang up. But in the tighter funding environment since, this rigid structure has become a liability. With a diminishing pool of graduate students on which to draw, promising offshoots with no power base are put in head-to-head competition with conventional, established work. An associate professor in biology who wishes to move into the new genetics, but whose department stresses classical biology, cannot go off on his own without taking money and students away from his colleagues. If he wants tenure, which is awarded by the department, he may hesitate before taking away his talent and the money and students which are the department's lifeblood.[13]

Moreover, agencies that divide themselves into neat disciplinary units make a national science policy impossible; for truly *national* science policy, almost by definition, crosses disciplinary lines.

Smith and Karlesky, in their still-relevant 1977 study of the impacts of level funding on university science, explain the stultifying impact of traditional university departments. For example, of the physics departments they visited, some of the "strong" departments (as opposed to ones rated "excellent") were having trouble attracting motivated graduate students. To keep the research going, one department converted itself to an institute-type operation and hired technicians to take the place of students. Some of the "good" and "adequate plus" physics departments were having difficulty justifying their large faculties relative to the small number of graduate students they were attracting. Many were having difficulty getting research grants — but of course trying to stay in the game. Several were going into short-term fusion and plasma physics research because money was available. (It is not obvious that, in a "good" or "adequate plus" physics department, this helps plasma physics, fusion research, or the parent university. All it does do is perpetuate the department and the faculty.)[14]

Indeed, a standard refrain that Smith and Karlesky heard from university scientists and department heads was how terrible it was that they were having to turn to applied research to keep going. The prevalence of this complaint, even at mid- and lower-ranked schools, shows how much the entire system, including the Jonesboro-type schools, has come to share the basic-research-is-best mindset, and how deep are the expectations of a perpetual handout to play the high-science game.[15] Another telling moment was when Smith and Karlesky were told by departments that had received NSF Science Development Grants to improve the "excellence" of their research (i.e., to aspire to the high science game) how hard they were being let down now that their Science Development Grants had ended and they had to compete openly for funding.

Smith and Karlesky's profile of the system in the late 1970s concluded that the cutthroat competition for funds was causing scientists to avoid taking risks; they were not giving creative chances to the younger scientists, thus compromising their future. What Smith and Karlesky described was not only a phenomenon of the 1970s, for the rising costs of scientific instruments and a likely decline in student population will create similar conditions for the rest of the century, even if budgets continue their present modest rise.

If we could design the system from scratch, we would not allow university departments in the traditional disciplines to gobble up new research topics and reshape them on their own Procrustean beds. Instead, we would use the enormous leverage of federal funds to encourage reform in universities to emphasize fluidity, creative, risk-taking work, and teamwork among specialists in different disciplines. We would try to enable university researchers to move back and forth between basic and applied problems.

In a reconfigured system applied work would not be done in a fragmentary way to keep the faculty employed until they can resume the high-science game. Instead, the majority of mid- and lower-ranked colleges and universities would reconfigure themselves to do *good* long-term applied science, concentrating on fields needed by local industry.

Confusion about freedom and accountability. The third structural issue we will take up in detail is the scientists' confusion about freedom and accountability. *Science—The Endless Frontier* argued that science could be entrusted with taxpayers' funds because it would (a) be self-governing and (b) give back results in terms of inventions and new industries, as it had during the war. This philosophy has worked best from OMB's viewpoint in mission-oriented engineering projects such as the Apollo program and some of the better DOD projects such as the Poseidon-Polaris program. There has been likewise a steady flow of improvements in the parts of medical research that have evolved in close alliance with clinical problems. Many of these efforts have been, for practical purposes, self-governing—often because they were led by project "champions" who fended off bureaucratic and political intrusions. The old Bush contract between science, government, and society held.

But some research universities define freedom very differently. "Freedom" means freedom to pursue one's research whims, so long as they pass muster with those doing like-minded research. Freedom also means freedom from other standards of judgment, such as whether work in a subspecialty contributes to anything outside, or whether the work has useful applications in the real world or to national needs. Such judgments would be considered by many scientists today as an infringement on their "freedom."

In short, most prefer to "escape to the endless frontier" (a quip which happens to be the title of another Don Price paper). But the word accountability means something entirely different to the local federal accountants who reside on every major campus. To them accountability means: hours spent on a project, keeping strictly to budget categories, accounting for broken glassware. Accountability does not mean whether the goal of the grant has been achieved.

Our critique, then, is that these long-standing structural weaknesses have fragmented university research into ever-more irrelevant parts in the name of basic-research-is-best. The system's defenders argue that university research should be isolated from tests of relevance to other fields, industry's needs, and society. While we agree that universities should take a more reflective view, this is no excuse for doing second-rate science because it follows the path of least resistance provided by the system.

A key development that may change the system is the new partnerships between universities and industry which have sprung up in recent years. Much hailed as a new source of income to universities (because the sums are sometimes large by ordinary grant standards) and publicized for the legal and ethical issues they raise (which are often satisfactorily solved), these partnerships have become a new vogue. To us they are welcome, and our reform of the system would have many more such partnerships and even allow industry in a region to help set university priorities.

But this reform is a long way off. Despite the hoopla, even our top universities receive only 3 to 4 percent of their income from industry, according to a 1982 National Science Board report. Only universities with long traditions of industry service are doing better: Carnegie-Mellon ranked first with 17.1 percent; next came the University of Rochester at 11.9 percent; Penn State, Georgia Tech, and the University of Southern California had 10 to 11 percent. But Harvard had only 4 percent; Princeton, 1.5 percent; and the University of Chicago, 0.7 percent. By 1983 industry contributed only 5 percent of all university research support.[16]

V

Many scientists may dismiss our critique on the grounds that the Reagan administration has been a booster for science. After a shaky start in fiscal 1981, the administration has continued increases in the basic research funding of the Carter administration, as Figure 6 shows. It can also be argued that the administration's economic policies, which have been to encourage research and development (R&D) investment, fuel an economic recovery (albeit through historically high deficits), and restore business confidence, have done more for the national R&D picture than any tinkering with the federal science budget could. Finally, Keyworth, the President's Science Adviser (though one of the few scientists *not* from the university world to hold the job), has turned out to be a public booster of science and technology — boosterism, to be sure, of an old-fashioned kind that would seem more appropriate for his boss, but boosterism nonetheless.[17]

For U.S. scientists to accept that U.S. research is healthy because this trend line is working in favor of university basic research is a narrow and probably irresponsible view. Who can be sanguine when the numbers of U.S. citizens opting to get the Ph.D. in the hard sciences is dwindling? The thousands of foreign graduate students now swelling our schools are welcome — especially as they compensate for level overall college enrollments — but this is not quite the same. And what does industry offer that university science does not to attract science graduates in such droves? The answer may be job stability, better pay, and perhaps the hope of a more rational career ladder ahead. These demographics, discussed further in Chapter 4, make up the human factor that should trouble U.S. scientists today. And they are structural problems that more funds for basic research cannot, in the end, cure.

Moreover, the Reagan administration has chillingly favored clamping down on academic freedom in the name of national

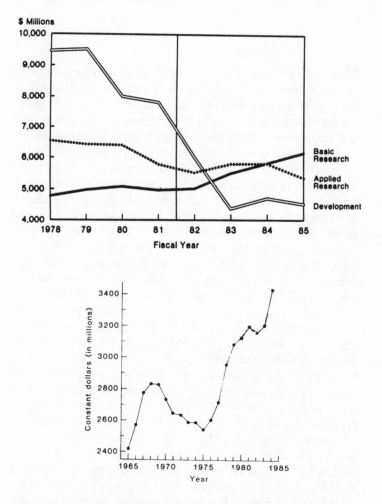

Figure 6 The science policy of the Reagan administration epitomizes many postwar trends in federal research and development funding. (*top*) The administration's insouciance for the fate of development projects and applied science is shown, in terms of federal research and development obligations in civilian areas, 1978–1985. Data in constant 1983 dollars. (*bottom*) Federal funding for basic research 1965–1985 in constant 1983 dollars. Recent increases are evident. (SOURCE: Office of Science and Technology Policy.)

security — even to the point of trying to stop a number of unclassified papers from being given at a large international meeting. While it has shown signs of backing off from a plan to restrict unclassified research that was thought to fall in "gray areas" of possible military significance, the administration's attitude may nonetheless be having a "chilling" effect on university research.

Thus, Keyworth's tenure has been a mixed bag. On the one hand, there is boosterism for basic research; on the other, a blithe willingness to axe federal applied science development and demonstration programs, including many of obvious, long-term, bipartisan importance, such as the Department of Energy's conservation research or the National Bureau of Standards' fire and building studies. As he wields the scalpel, Keyworth declares that if there is worthy development work to be done, private industry should do it (defense projects should be the exception, he adds).

With reference to our theme in this essay, Keyworth represents a step backwards, to the old basic-research-is-best attitude which assumes that American research must be all right if basic research has funds. In his cutting of federal applied science, he is ignoring the need for linkage with the federal science system.

On the other hand, his willingness to experiment with the institutions of the postwar science establishment is long overdue. At first Keyworth sounded as though he would close down or spin off the national laboratories — the large federal centers that sprang up in Bush's day and live on, like woolly mammoths foraging for food as the glaciers advance. He has encouraged the new trend toward industry–university partnerships — which, despite much publicity, are only a tiny fraction of the university research picture. He has responded to calls from Congress to do more in engineering by establishing engineering centers run by the NSF (meanwhile fighting off attempts by Congress to give the NSF a major science educational role). There is a new panel headed by David Packard on the structure and funding of federal science. These experiments we applaud, for they offer a faint glimmer of hope that old institutions and values, entrenched for 30 years, may change after all.

NOTES

[1] J. Merton England, *A Patron for Pure Science: The National Foundation's Formative Years, 1945-57* (Washington, D.C.: National Science Foundation) 82-14368, p. 109.

[2] *Ibid.*, p. 100.

[3] Alice Kimball Smith, *A Peril and A Hope* (Chicago: University of Chicago Press, 1965), pp. 273, 274, 267, and Chaps. 13 and 14.

[4] Daniel J. Kevles, *The Physicists, The History of a Scientific Community in Modern America* (New York: Alfred A. Knopf, 1978), pp. 354-356, 359. Author interview with Willis H. Shapley, formerly of the Bureau of the Budget.

[5] Daniel S. Greenberg, *The Politics of Pure Science* (New American Library, reprint Plume Books, 1967), pp. 133, 134; England, *op. cit.*, pp. 141-155.

[6] Greenberg, *op. cit.*, pp. 133, 134 and p. 121.

[7] England, *op. cit.*, pp. 348, 349.

[8] *Ibid.*, p. 361.

[9] Paul E. Gray, "M.I.T. and Industry: A Partnership," in *The Decades Ahead, an M.I.T. Perspective*, Proceedings of a symposium for senior executives, 24-26 June 1980, Industrial Liaison Program of M.I.T., p. 130.

[10] A. Kantrowitz, "Leadership in Applied Physical Science," *Basic Research and National Goals* (Washington, D.C.: National Academy of Sciences, 1965), pp. 143-44.

[11] Hendrik W. Bode, "Reflections on the Relation Between Science and Technology," *Basic Research and National Goals* (Washington, D.C.: National Academy of Sciences, 1965), pp. 74, 75.

[12] Barry Bozeman and Dong Kim, "Governing the Republic of Science: an Analysis of National Science Foundation Officials' Attitudes about Managed Science," in *Polity*, Vol. XIV, No. 2, Winter 1981, pp. 183-204.

[13] Bruce L. R. Smith and Joseph J. Karlesky, *The State of Academic Science* (New York: Change Magazine Press, 1971), Vol. I, p. 142.

[14] *Ibid.*, pp. 102-117, esp. 113, 114.

[15] *Ibid.*, Chap. 4.

[16] *Science Indicators 1982* (Washington, D.C.: National Science Board, 1983), pp. 107, 127.

[17] See, for example, text of Keyworth remarks at R&D Policy Colloquium, AAAS, 29 March 1984, and remarks at National Academy of Sciences Dinner for Nobel Laureates, 8 March 1984.

3

Industrial Research Adrift

As IN 1945, TODAY the United States is poised on the threshold of another industrial revolution. In 1945 electronics, polymeric chemicals, new pharmaceuticals, and aviation were ushering in the previous industrial revolution. Today, small computers, fiber optics, robotics, laser and plasma processing of semiconductors, new metals, ceramics, and molecular genetics are ushering in the next one. Through science and technology, we can almost see into the future.

Yet few people understand that for the United States to get to the next industrial revolution, let alone prosper in it, will not be simple. Turn on the spigot for basic research funds, cry the university scientists, and you will get innovation and prosperity. Pass a national industrial policy, cry some economists: it will push us into the future. Fix management, say the business consultants. It is hardly surprising that as the country faces universal, troubling problems of social, industrial, and technological change, everyone with a soapbox has his or her own right answer.

The many books and articles about how industry should adjust say remarkably little about industrial research. Indeed, the literature illustrates the divorce between science and the real world that we are criticizing in this essay. The management consultants and industrial policy advocates all treat the march of technology in the same old wrongheaded fashion, namely, that technology marches inexorably forward as part of what Derek deSolla Price called the "great chain of being" that starts with science.

This essay is concerned with the great gulf between science and applications that has been encouraged by the science profession's fixation on the specialness of basic research. In the previous chapter we saw how it permeated federal science institutions and the universities. In this chapter we consider how the same attitude has hurt industry, for industry too often treats science as a separate ivory tower activity, unconnected to anything else. When times became tough in the 1970s, industry cut back on much of its long-term applied and purposive basic research while stepping up near-term development work on known products.

We argue that it is possible for an industrial organization to have good basic science and innovate at the same time. Close coupling between science and applications can help both, contrary to the science profession's myth. This chapter will look, first, at the premier example of this synergism in industry, AT&T Bell Laboratories, which has had an outstanding track record in producing Nobel Prize winners and doing applied science and development for the phone company. Second, it will look at the outstanding weakness of the U.S. industrial research system, its lack of coordination with the government, and describe instances of good coordination (the old agricultural research system) and bad coordination (ceramic engines).

Finally, it will discuss management styles for research in an industrial organization. Solving the problems in the linkage between science and the introduction of new products is no easy matter. It deserves many books of its own. Nonetheless, we discuss it here because it represents yet another problem in getting U.S. science to serve broad national ends.

I

U.S. industrial research has been through three phases since 1945. In the first, industry was enamored of research. As Vannevar Bush wrote in 1945 in *Science—The Endless Frontier*, the postwar industries were more closely tied to science than had been Henry Ford's auto business or Thomas A. Edison's electric power network. After the war, U.S. corporations built impressive research arms: many became synonymous with quality research in their various fields such as General Electric, Du Pont, and Bell Laboratories. The Big Three U.S. automakers were credited with knowing more about cars than anyone else in the world. A company's stock was worth more the more it spent on R&D; the cover of its annual report often sported a picture of a lavish research laboratory campus. This growth was the analog of the growth of federally sponsored university research described previously.

In this phase, industry mimicked the idolatry of basic research that was evolving in the federal–university science system. U.S. Steel and Ford, among others, built flashy basic research laboratories that purported to show — wrongly, as it turned out — that their respective companies would be at the forefront of technological development. The laboratories even bragged about how independent they were from the company, imitating the proud isolationism of university science. The General Electric laboratory at Schenectady, New York, the Rockwell Science Center at Thousand Oaks, California, and similar places rightly claimed that they offered university-type settings; they shared the universities' defects as well.

In phase two, times were harder, and many companies abandoned these efforts because they lacked a commitment to the science and often didn't know how to transfer the knowledge in the laboratory to the production line in the first place. The laboratories which were exceptions then remain exceptional today; outstanding examples are Bell Laboratories and IBM. Each had a strong commitment to linking basic and applied research; each was large enough to instill lasting corporate habits and sustain them through hard times.

U.S. Steel is an example of the problem. It built a big basic research laboratory whose scientists acquired a unique instrument, a million-volt electron microscope with which they did basic research looking at structure at the atomic level. As far as we can tell, the laboratory never gave priority of any kind to the critical applied area that was revolutionizing the steel industry worldwide: this was the process metallurgy which led to the more efficient "Austrian" method of steelmaking. Eventually, U.S. Steel had to license the new method from abroad, perhaps 10 years after its own scientists could have really helped the company by giving priority to such applied areas. Not surprisingly, U.S. Steel later discontinued its basic research effort.

Industrial basic research had as hard a time with level funding as did the federal–university system. Many companies, especially those in regulated industries, gave up all pretense of doing long-term research in favor of refining existing products. This falling away of industry's commitment was a natural (but insidious) consequence of the postwar science system. Industrial managers had been too caught up in the next quarter's bottom line, and in worrying about regulatory issues, to learn the underlying technologies on which their businesses were based. Management expert Peter F. Drucker wrote of the conglomerates:

> Yesterday's business, organized around a process, such as making glass, was basically technologically oriented and therefore looked to science for its future. The conglomerate, which comprises everything from tin cans and electronics to fast food restaurants and dress shops, from airlines to banks and toys, is, of necessity, financially oriented. *Research becomes a cost center rather than a producer of tomorrow's wealth* [emphasis added].[1]

The industrial culture Drucker describes was ubiquitous (except in small, research-intensive corporations and in a few large ones). Its values mirrored those of the federal–university system where science chose to be treated as a self-contained sector, best left to itself. Of course, such attitudes by managers, marketing, and production people are abetted when even the R&D staff share them. In too many corporations, scientists and engineers had the same narrow view of their role we have seen in the federal-university system. They did not want to be responsible for applications; applications meant whether or not the company succeeds. The leave-me-alone, ask-no-questions attitude of university basic researchers helped undermine industrial research as well. Some symptoms of the trouble, including the declining U.S. patent balance, are shown in Figure 7.

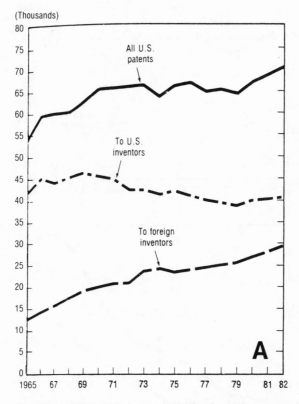

Figures 7A, 7B, and 7C U.S. industrial technology, the supposed fruit of our national research effort, is in trouble, according to three key indicators.

Figure 7A Overall U.S. inventiveness appears to be declining, both absolutely and in relation to foreign inventiveness, as measured by the number of U.S. patents granted to U.S. and foreign inventors, by date of application and year, as shown. (SOURCE: *Science Indicators 1982*, Figure 4-8, p. 101.)

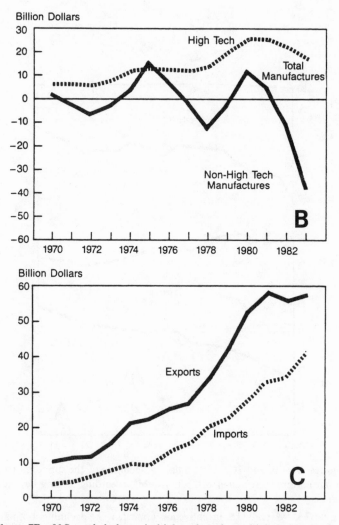

Figure 7B U.S. trade balance in high-tech and non-high-tech manufactures, 1970–1983. For years, the United States has relied on its positive high-technology trade balance to compensate for the poor return from sales of non-high-technology products. Yet this key indicator has been declining since 1980 (and continued to decline through June 1984, according to Department of Commerce data). An important feature of this

The third phase began in the late 1970s. Industry began hiring more and more scientists and engineers each year, a trend which has continued since. The total R&D spending by industry began to rise gradually and accelerated after the Reagan administration took office. The overall numbers are rising: has industry rediscovered the importance of science?

The trend was due to several outside factors whose impact, however, is hard to document. Most companies held on to their development activities as a result of government regulation. As long-term work dropped off, it was compensated for by increased development work on known products to meet regulations.

Then in 1981 came the Economic Recovery Tax Act, which permitted more write-offs for R&D expenses.[2] The act may have caused more industrial R&D spending, but it also spurred bookkeeping changes in which other ongoing activities were redefined as R&D. While some companies made conspicuous new research efforts, the existence of a "rediscovery" of the kind of long-term research that could revolutionize industrial technology is still in doubt.

Finally came the Reagan administration's defense budget, which pumped into the aerospace and electronics industries huge sums of money and caused the federally supported "D" component of industrial R&D to rise still more. One interesting indicator is the very modest growth in the amount of their own money companies were plowing into research.[3] This indicator was one of the

---

indicator is that it includes foreign military sales, which have risen in the Reagan administration. Yet despite this rise, the overall decline is marked. (SOURCE: U.S. Trade, Performance in 1983 and Outlook, U.S. Department of Commerce, International Trade Administration, June 1984, Figure 3.1, p. 13.)

Figure 7C U.S. high-tech exports and imports, 1970–1983. The reasons for the declining high-technology trade balance are evident: U.S. imports of foreign high-technology products are rising relative to exports. U.S. consumers and companies appear to be preferring foreign high-technology products to those made in the United States. Such imports continued to increase through June 1984, even as U.S. exports declined, according to Department of Commerce data. (SOURCE: U.S. Trade, Performance in 1983 and Outlook, op. cit., Figure 3.2, p. 15.)

engines that fueled our technical lead after the war. In the 1977–1980 period, industry's funding of its own R&D rose at 7.3 percent per year in constant dollars. But the increases were expected to drop subsequently, as a result of uncertain economic conditions, companies' preference for letting their rivals assume risks, and management's preference for short-term work, sure to pay off, over riskier long-range R&D.

In this third phase, too, the U.S. biotechnology industry became capitalized; hundreds of small firms were able to raise surprisingly large sums from private investors and stock sales. The glamour of the biotechnology area masked, however, much more modest increases in more traditional industrial fields. And the boom seemed likely to land with a loud thump.

Thus, the overall trend of lack of support of long-term basic and applied research in industry may not have changed much from the sad situation of the 1970s.

One result, in basic physics, is shown in Figure 8. There was a time when some industrial research laboratories were the peers of their university counterparts, even in physics. But a recent analysis of contributors to *Physical Review Letters*, the most prestigious basic research journal in physics, shows that fewer and fewer industry physicists have published there. By 1979, only two corporations, Bell Laboratories and IBM, accounted for nearly three-fourths of the industrial papers published in *Physical Review Letters*. The study made an equally dismal finding for industrial contributors to *Applied Physics Letters*. The same number of U.S. industry-supported papers were published in *Applied Physics Letters* over a 13-year period, from 1966 to 1979. In view of the rising number of contributors from other sectors, this amounts to "near stagnation" in industrial applied physics. Industry's contribution is a "rapidly diminishing fraction of the whole U.S. contribution," according to Ted G. Berlincourt of the Office of Naval Research (ONR), who, with others, wrote the report.[4]

There has been a toll in engineering as well. American engineering in industry has been hurt by the university community's neglect of engineering as a whole. Tufts University President Jean Mayer has blamed U.S. industry's inability to build satisfactory nuclear power plants, subway cars, or probes for cybernetic sys-

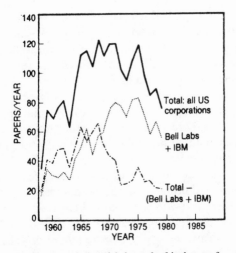

Figure 8 One indicator of the withdrawal of industry from its effort in basic research is its general decline in performed basic science during the decade of the 1970s, shown earlier in Figure 5 (Chapter 2). Another indicator, shown above, is the declining numbers of papers published by U.S. industry generally in the premier basic science journal of the field of physics, *Physical Review Letters*. The dotted line indicates that the contributions of Bell Laboratories and IBM grew until 1970 and declined, on average, since. The contributions of all other companies began to decline after 1968. (SOURCE: Ted G. Berlincourt, Harold Weinstock, Francis Narin, and Samuel G. Reischer, "Trends in Research Output and Funding," *Physics Today*, November 1982, Figure 1, p. 9.)

tems in the steel industry on the universities' lack of emphasis on engineering. He noted that most universities fail to give graduate engineers the kind of rigorous postgraduate training routinely given to doctors.[5]

If a nation builds a value system (reflected in its prizes, budgets, policy discussion, and the like) that downgrades engineering and applied science and makes engineers and applied scientists feel inferior to researchers in pure physics and biology, sooner or later that nation will get bad engineering and bad applied science, even though its pure biology or physics is terrific.

The lack of strong applied science and sound management of applied science could be considered a national crisis far more serious than the questions science policy analysts are fond of, such as whether the next year's federal outlays for basic research will rise by 8.5 percent or by 10 percent after inflation.

In industry, researchers have too little clout with management. An engineer at Ford with a brilliant concept may have no more hope of talking to Ford's president than the president of Ford may have of understanding him. Yet the auto industry must become technologically nimble to survive.

Our purpose in this essay is to call the science profession's attention to a critical problem of our national technological effort. *This is the need to create much more tightly interconnected systems centered on long-term applied research in U.S. industry, drawing on university and government laboratories as needed, to enable the United States to participate fully in the new industrial revolution.* Otherwise, U.S. science and technology could go the way of Great Britain, with an admirable small group of basic researchers who contribute fundamental advances, but bring few economic returns to the country. This result is the opposite of the one envisioned in *Science—The Endless Frontier.*

The major corporations that formed the backbone of U.S. postwar prosperity were built and run by technical people, inventor–entrepreneurs involved in the development of the core technology on which the company was based. Chester Carlson invented the dry copier, literally, in his kitchen and with Joseph Wilson turned it into Xerox Corporation; Bill Allen and Thornton Wilson built Boeing. Robert Noyce at Intel, Kenneth Olsen at Digital Equipment Corporation, William Hewlett, David Packard, and others put the United States ahead in electronics. Sometimes, as in the case of Edwin Land of Polaroid, the original technical genius has stayed on top for decades.

Now, without technical understanding at a very fundamental and sophisticated level, how can a chief executive officer (CEO) decide which of several competing technologies on the horizon is the right choice? Today and in future, CEOs will have to make *technological* decisions: how clever they are at anticipating technological change may well make the difference between a business' success or failure. Yet the older generation of inventor–entrepreneurs are passing from the scene. Five to nine percent of U.S. CEOs today have technical backgrounds, as defined by having once worked in engineering.[6] The U.S. chemical industry is healthier than most, with nearly 50 percent of its CEOs drawn from science and engineering; it stands out from the pack. Moreover, very few indeed are original inventor–entrepreneurs: it is one thing to merely get an engineering degree; it is another to have 537 patents to one's name, as Land did in 1984.

This is where management styles come in. As explained by two McKinsey & Co. consultants, Thomas J. Peters and Robert H. Waterman, Jr., in their book *In Search of Excellence*, "back to basics" is the latest trend in management thinking.[7] Its thesis (consistent with, but different from, ours) is that companies that stay "excellent" are those which stick to their knitting. These companies have developed a secure place in their core business and stayed with it, continually relearning it at all levels and getting continual feedback from customers — from the lowliest MacDonald's cashier to the president of Delta Airlines. But we will come to the Peters and Waterman view of management in the context of research shortly.

II

Before turning to Bell Laboratories and the problems of linking basic science and applications in industry, let us quickly review what is known about innovation. The literature on innovation shows in many, rich case histories that the better managed the links are, the more innovation occurs.

Studies of innovation have two flaws. The first is a tendency to aggregate data across industries and government programs. This tends to wipe out critical differences in sectors, markets, and technologies. Second, many of the studies strain to reach sweeping conclusions (usually about the need for federal support of basic research) while ignoring richer, more specific conclusions for applied science policy. If anyone were constructing an applied science policy for the United States, this literature is a good starting point.

The best known study of innovation was Project Hindsight,

published in 1965. In it the Department of Defense asked whether its then-large investment of $400 million a year in research—of which approximately one-fourth went for basic research—was paying off. The study looked at 20 defense systems and identified a total of 710 "events," often occurring as chains of events, that led to them. The conclusions reached by the authors are close to our own, and threatening to the defenders of basic-research-is-best. They noted that without fundamental science none of the innovations would have been possible. But

> it is unusual for random, disconnected fragments of scientific knowledge to find application rapidly. It is, rather, the evaluated, compressed, organized, interpreted and simplified scientific knowledge that we find to be the most effective connection between the undirected research laboratory and the world of practical affairs.[8]

The National Science Foundation (NSF) commissioned its own study, called TRACES, of the role of basic science in innovation. Completed shortly after Project Hindsight, it became a de facto attempt at rebuttal. It traced the origins of birth control pills, electron microscopes, videotape recording, cermet materials, and matrix isolation to find that, if lag times up to 30 years are allowed, undirected basic science played a key role. When an update was commissioned by the NSF, published in 1973, however, the key events leading to another set of innovations were found to be half mission-oriented and half basic research-oriented. But only fifteen of the "critical" events leading to the innovations fell into the basic science category.[9]

We will not speculate on the motives of those who commissioned the TRACES study and others like it, but we must note how convenient their findings were to the ideology of the federal–university system. If the public pays for science because, possibly, 30 years from now (and long after today's recipients have passed from the scene), it just *might* prove useful (but no one can predict exactly how, and anarchy-serendipity is useful), then both patron and recipient are absolved of responsibility for the results. Thus, this reasoning goes, science should be isolated from responsibility for applications.

On the other hand, if it were admitted that research *does* have near-term applications, especially when "evaluated, compressed, organized, interpreted and simplified" to be an "effective connection . . . to the world of practical affairs," as the Project Hindsight authors wrote, then the patron and recipients of federal research dollars face a much more demanding task and heavier responsibilities. They could not just take the government's money and divide it up by quaint procedures. They would have to worry — as industrial scientists in the best companies do — about how and where their work would show some value.

Fortunately, the ideology of the 1960s, which seized on studies like TRACES as proof of the basic-research-is-best view, has moderated of late. Some of today's scientists may feel sheepish that approximately 40 years after this remarkable investment by the federal government began, which was to lead automatically to great industrial productivity, the United States has been bested by Japan in a number of technology-intensive industries. They have been forced to admit that there must be more to achieving industrial excellence than federal support of basic science!

The economists are changing too. Richard R. Nelson of Yale University writes that a decade ago most economists subscribed to the idea that federal support of basic research was of itself an appropriate policy to foster innovation. Now, he writes, they tend more to recognize that other policies may also be important.[10]

III

Bell Laboratories (now called AT&T Bell Laboratories, Inc., since the break-up of the telephone company monopoly on 1 January 1984) has been a powerful exception to the science profession's mythology about the divorce between basic science and applications. Its basic science has been outstanding by any standard; work done for the laboratories has garnered four Nobel Prizes shared among seven winners. Yet, in seeming contradiction it has served as the development arm of the telephone company and has been under constant pressure to improve products.

Bell Laboratories grew up when the telephone system did, and its first president (1925–1940), Frank B. Jewett, was previously chief engineer for Western Electric. Jewett made his early mark on the company by organizing the first trans-continental telephone service for the Panamerican–Pacific exposition in California in 1915.

The telephone company needed a laboratory because it needed technology. "Watson, come here" may have signaled the invention of a telephone that could work between rooms, but radio telephony had to replace wires as the system grew. The postwar explosion in demand for service required microwave links between cities, and each subsequent stage demanded greater quantity and quality of service.[11]

Thus the company exerted a strong pull on the laboratories, for it had an overwhelming need for innovations. And Bell Laboratories kept producing them: over the horizon radio, digital transmission, light wave transmission, and many others.

Jewett believed that groups of scientists and engineers working in concert got more done than the same people working independently, so he structured Bell Laboratories to have pluralistic, but nonetheless group, approaches to problems. Ease of communications among employees was considered essential. Intellectual competition face-to-face was better than people working alone, he believed. To this day, even new or junior staff are instructed to pick up the telephone (!) and call anyone else — even people they don't know and people far their senior — to ask for technical advice or information.[12]

This collegiality is a feature of their peer review system too. Any individual or team can write up some work and circulate the paper internally. Not only does this tell others what is being done but it also gives the author feedback from everyone, including those not working in his particular subject area. Instead of being published outside, the test of merit is praise (or criticism) from other staff.

The fact that Bell Laboratories' "bosses" (namely AT&T and Western Electric, which own Bell Laboratories 50–50, even after the breakup) were an entire *system*, and not just a single-product company, seems to have left an institutional mark. Bell Laboratories had to come up with the "systems" design for the telephone network: systems engineering became ingrained into management's style.

So it was that in the 1930s, when Mervin J. Kelly determined that mechanical switches could not handle the growing volume of traffic in the system's switching stations, a search was launched for some technology, preferably electronic, to replace them. Vacuum tubes were one possibility; William Shockley and others thought semiconductive materials might serve. Shockley's early attempt failed; if he had been working under the current U.S. federal–university system, he might not have obtained a follow-on grant to his first one because things hadn't worked out. The fundamental reasons it had failed were unknown, and would remain so for a long time.

But Bell Laboratories persisted, and in 1947, Walter Brittain and John Bardeen stumbled on the transistor effect in a particular germanium single crystal that had been purified and grown by the materials science group. Theory would not have predicted this result; the discovery of the effect in this particular crystal was the synergistic result of the work on materials. Their result led Shockley to come up with another design that became the transistor. It ushered in the electronics revolution, which transformed both the communications and electronics industries.

Now, if Bell Laboratories had been an ordinary university science department, Shockley's early negative result might have caused the work to be dropped, so that he could move on to some other, more productive problem. It would be unlikely for a university group to still be persisting 8 years later, in any event. Nor would Gordon Teal at Bell Laboratories have necessarily spent another 2 years trying to find a commercially viable method for growing single crystals of germanium so transistors could be mass produced: Shockley's device had been unsuitable for mass production.

In the rest of the story, the science/engineering/technology coupling was very close. In 1953 Teal took his invaluable know-how to Texas Instruments and began a program for silicon for transistors, giving that company a 3-year head start in the silicon semiconductor field. Western Electric and the receiving-tube suppliers jumped to get in on the ground floor of the revolution. One tribute to the flexibility of the receiving-tube companies is that they garnered no less than 40 percent of the key early patents.[13]

The military was such an obvious customer for the invention

that Bell Laboratories did not tell the military about it at first, for fear it would be classified and prohibited from commercial use. The Navy leaped in with its own work, obtaining more of the relevant patents than any other military service.

The later evolution both of discrete device transistors and of integrated circuitry is full of the same synergisms which pushed the entire field through its amazing revolution, and drove semiconductors through their amazing descent in size and cost and their accompanying increase in reliability.[14]

The birth of radio astronomy at Bell Laboratories is, from its point of view, an example of this "systems engineering" approach producing both technology and science. The desire to provide overseas telephone service required long-distance radio transmission and reception. So every kind of radio noise had to be investigated. Among others, Karl G. Jansky, who had started with Bell Laboratories in 1928 at the age of 22, was involved in the classification of this noise. In 1932 he found three types: noise from local thunderstorms, noise from distant thunderstorms, and a steady "hiss." A colleague who knew some astronomy dismissed it, but Jansky was fascinated by the noise and persisted in investigating it.

It took a radio amateur to confirm Jansky's discovery that the "hiss" came from the stars. The discovery, in effect, founded radio astronomy, and indirectly, millimeter wave spectroscopy by which we now study the molecules deep in space. Yet while engaged in this incredible discovery, Jansky became an expert in the very applied business of where to locate transmission sites for the company.

These anecdotes may explain why Bell Laboratories, whose work today is 90 percent development and only 10 percent research, credits the fact that it *is* tied to a commercial organization, and *is* under pressure to produce applications, as the reason it has done good science. One text reads:

How many Bell Laboratories discoveries and developments would have been made if there had been no Bell System of which the Laboratories could be a part? It is inconceivable that the depth and range of achievement could have been as great. For what equally productive organization could have functioned somewhere off in limbo, busily creating — what? Every creative institution needs clearly defined purposes. Those of Bell Laboratories have been compelling.[15]

Needless to say, this wisdom flies in the face of the ideology of university science in the United States for the past 30 years!

IV

The synergism we saw at Bell Laboratories is found in other research systems that have been continually innovative over a long period of time.

The story of U.S. agriculture, we argue, illustrates the point. It shows that not only can basic research and continuous new product innovations go hand in hand, but that the *government* can even aid in the process. The old U.S. agricultural research system, in which the "industry" of farmers, farm suppliers (such as seed companies), and food companies all made use of federal and regional research, was an interesting case of this kind of synergism. Although by now somewhat decrepit, for a century it innovated continuously across a wide spectrum of products.

We left off with U.S. agriculture in our first chapter, in noting that Vannevar Bush believed that the system of agricultural experiment stations and land-grant colleges, established in the nineteenth century, should be the model for postwar U.S. science institutions. By 1945 the gains had been impressive, and were rooted in science. Bush wrote:

> Great advances in agriculture are also based upon scientific research. Plants which are more resistant to disease and are adapted to short growing seasons, the prevention and cure of livestock diseases, the control of our insect enemies, better fertilizers and improved agricultural practices, all stem from painstaking scientific research.[16]

After the war, these advances would continue and multiply —

aided by an increase in federally sponsored agricultural research that came with postwar government largesse. Table 1 illustrates the impact of these advances on some important crops.

The system works thus: Research is carried out by more than fifty State Agricultural Experiment Stations (SAES) and Department of Agriculture research centers at local universities. These are also training grounds for students, many of whom will become farmers or researchers. Technology transfer occurs through the county agent who visits the area's farmers, communicating recent results. States support this system on a formula basis, with matching federal funds. These government funds are equalled by industry spending on research, which has grown with each passing decade. The fantastic productivity gains per acre shown in Table 1 are possible because the farmer is experimenter, consumer, and producer both of the research and, in some cases, of the goods. The farmer tests new seed varieties, techniques, and breeding practices that emerge from the SAES and Department of Agriculture research; the farmer similarly tests out machinery, herbicides, pesticides, and other supplier improvements. The SAES and county agents act as continual evaluators of the performance of new products and techniques.

This continuous feedback loop has another educational component in the land-grant colleges. These do research and train farmers. In effect, they transfer technology know-how through people. For most of their history, they have been prevented from becoming too high-science oriented, or too far behind each other, by the political pressure that the farm constituencies exert on the schools through state legislatures.[17]

The agricultural research system in its heyday had features similar to those of Bell Laboratories, in fact. The most obvious one is continuous feedback loops between the customer–user of the product and the research organization. Before the telephone company breakup, AT&T included all the telephone operating companies in the country; Western Electric sold its high-technology products (which emanated in part from Bell Laboratories) to military and civilian customers. AT&T and Western Electric could make the experience of the product known to the research staff who could modify it or try another iteration. The

Table 1 The U.S. agricultural research system innovated continuously over a long period (1915–1980), bringing about the remarkable decline in labor inputs and growth in yields shown below*

Years	Hours per acre	Yield, bushels	Hours per 100 bushels
CORN FOR GRAIN			
1915–19	34.2	25.9	132
1925–29	30.3	26.3	115
1935–39	28.1	26.1	108
1945–49	19.2	36.1	53
1955–59	9.9	48.7	20
1965–69	5.8	78.5	7
1976–80	3.5	96.0	4
SORGHUM GRAIN			
1925–29	17.5	16.8	104
1935–39	13.1	12.8	102
1945–49	8.8	17.8	49
1955–59	5.9	29.2	20
1965–69	4.2	52.9	8
1976–80	3.8	53.8	7
WHEAT			
1915–19	13.6	13.9	98
1925–29	10.5	14.1	74
1935–39	8.8	13.2	67
1945–49	5.7	16.9	34
1955–59	3.8	22.3	17
1965–69	2.9	27.5	11
1976–80	2.8	32	9

* Data from R. R. Nelson, ed., *Government and Technical Progress, A Cross-Industry Analysis* (New York: Pergamon Press, 1982), Table 5.2, p. 238.

Bell system has the equivalent of the agricultural system's county agents in its "branch laboratories" at five locations around the country. At these, regular laboratory staff work with the operating companies directly.

While the agricultural research system is far more differentiated locally (researchers in Florida study orange growing;

researchers in Kansas study wheat and corn), and the Bell system is centralized, both have remarkable incentives to get innovations distributed into the field. In Bell's case, it is the need for uniformity, i.e., there is no point in installing better microwave links only in New England. In the agricultural research system, if the farm lobby in one state sees improved corn and wheat growing in the next, it will put political pressure on its own agricultural researchers to do better.

What makes both dramatically different from the postwar university science community's paradigm for research and innovation is the existence of *organizational mechanisms* for linking the research effort to the customer. Both Bell and the agricultural research system set up places for scientists to work and give them money, as the federal science system does. But our two examples go several steps further in organizing a continuous flow of linkages and feedback loops between the research activity and the user.

Today, the agricultural research system has become bogged down by the narrow interests of its constituencies. Agriculture is politically popular at the state and federal levels. It has been easy to parcel out more money to various branches of the system at the urging of the powerful lobby groups. There is no powerful counterbalance that can speak for the integrity of the research itself, that can speak for excellence and innovation over political pork barrel (a problem, we have seen, with many federal development demonstration programs). It shares the problem of weak central management that is a trademark of the federal science system. And it lacks, for practical purposes, the "systems engineering" approach that guides research, both basic and applied, at Bell Laboratories.

It is not surprising that, today, the agricultural research system is under attack by the university science community. Recently, it has had grounds.[18] The biotechnology revolution has been transforming agricultural science. The revolution in genetics enables the invention of new seeds, the breeding of farm animals with desirable characteristics, and crops resistant to disease and infestation. All this has occurred largely outside the now-cumbersome, politicized agricultural system. Federal science officials and others have been struggling with the hardest problem of all: institutional reform. But, it seems, the simplistic answer so far is that old war cry, "More money for basic research."

Besides agriculture, aviation has been an area of federal–industry coupling through the National Advisory Committee for Aeronautics (NACA), established at the time of World War I. This was the agency Vannevar Bush headed at the outset of World War II; it later became the nucleus of the National Aeronautics and Space Administration (NASA).

In its wind tunnels and laboratories, NACA conducted both basic and applied research, guided by committees made up of representatives of industry, the military services, and university-based aeronautical scientists and engineers. A pattern of collaboration grew up which provided the technical basis for the success of the U.S. aircraft industry, civilian and military. All sides agreed that the government would do research (usually involving costly facilities such as wind tunnels) which advancing technology required but which none of the companies could carry out separately. As noted in Chapter 1, NACA's mission was the "scientific study of the problems of flight with a view to their practical solution." Basic research was not neglected: on the contrary, it was carried out in the context of applications.

Although eclipsed by the larger scale and greater visibility of space activities after 1958, when NASA was formed, aeronautical research has continued in the old NACA tradition. Keyworth only belatedly found it a model of government–industry cooperation in research: once marked for extinction in the Reagan administration's vendetta against federally funded applied research, Keyworth's office mounted a study which not only recommended sparing it but reaffirmed its terms in a surprising policy reversal.[19] NASA's good record in coordinating industry and government research and technology development probably derives in part from its inheritance of the NACA tradition. Certainly this tradition helped the U.S. aviation industry hold its stunning world lead through half a century.

Now to a story about how *not* to try to put the United States ahead in a "hot" research field. This is the case of ceramics — a field in which one of us is deeply involved and has seen first-hand the United States' inability to allocate government–industry roles. Crash government programs followed by nothing and faddish industry interest characterize the story. Needless to say, the Japanese, who saw the potential of ceramics to make lighter weight and more fuel-efficient engines at the time we did, are moving ahead more effectively.

But it is the U.S. side of the story that concerns us here.

The 1950s, 1960s, and 1970s saw the phenomenal growth of plastics (polymers) as a useful technology. In 30 years the volume of polymers produced outstripped that of metals; much of the growth has come at the expense of metals. But polymers require petroleum, whose availability and cost are problematic. Ceramics are inorganic, nonmetallic materials. Glass and fine porcelain are the familiar middle-tech version of ceramics. The synthetic rubies used in lasers and the glass fibers used in fiber optics are the best known high-tech ceramics. Since ceramics are made of the commonest elements on earth, no questions of availability or price can arise. Moreover, they have many advantages over metals.

In the early 1970s, various corporate and national groups abroad began exploring the best ways to develop ceramics. There was no group in the United States which could conduct such an analysis, let alone make a plan. Two corporations formed the total U.S. technology base exclusively focused on ceramics: Carborundum in Niagara Falls, New York, and Norton in Worcester, Massachusetts. Coors Porcelain, 3M, and General Electric had substantial ceramic interests too.

The U.S. government seized on ceramics for defense uses after an American postdoc, Fred Lange, returned from Harwell in Great Britain to join Westinghouse and brought news of British success with silicon nitride. Possibly it was *the* material for a turbine engine running at much higher temperatures than any metal can achieve. On the basis of vague data from Britain, the Advanced Research Projects Agency (ARPA) decided to go for broke, skip the basic and applied science stages, and quickly demonstrate a fully engineered ceramic turbine engine in 5 years! The oil shock of 1973 appeared to confirm the wisdom of this choice. The Department of Energy (DOE) entered the develop-

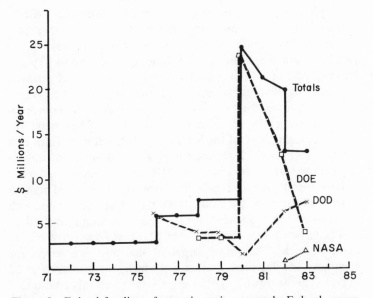

Figure 9 Federal funding of ceramic engine research. Federal government science policy, preoccupied with maintenance of a steady flow of funds for basic research, has little capability to organize and manage civilian applied science, development, and demonstration programs, leading to chronic instability in many. A glaring example, illustrated here, was the Department of Defense's sudden leap to develop a ceramic engine in 1976, an ill-conceived effort that resulted in the program's near-termination. Later, the Department of Energy leaped into the field; still later, the National Aeronautics and Space Administration became involved. This instability may be a factor in Japan's lead in the field. (SOURCE: Joshua Lerner, based on data from DOD, DOE, and NASA.)

ment game too, but lacked coordination with the Department of Defense.

But the Reagan Administration cut the DOE's program in half one year and to one-fifth the next. As Figure 9 shows, U.S. government R&D on the ceramic engine went through an enormous spike and down again. How can technology gestate under these conditions?

The first major failure of this effort was mislabeling. ARPA and DOE mistook ceramic engines for all of ceramics. Yet there is a multi-billion dollar electronic ceramics industry, whereas the first commercial ceramic engine will not be sold for 5 to 10 years. We were putting all our research energies into a far off product, and ignoring obvious research to advance key, present products.

Needless to say, the Japanese took a long hard look at the problem; discussion took place between the Agency of Industrial Science and Technology of the Ministry of International Trade and Industry (MITI), the many industries large and small, and university commentators. By March of 1978 they had developed a national research plan for the development of the advanced high-efficiency gas turbine. A parallel effort by the Engineering Research Association was launched with fourteen companies involved.

The "fine ceramics" program of MITI was part of a second planning cycle. The prime target of this push was electronic ceramics — the Japanese market for which was estimated at $2 billion. The worldwide figures are several times this amount.

Now, U.S. industry is agitated about the "opening" toward ceramics. One of us has been visited by more than two dozen of the nation's leading corporations asking how best they should enter the field. Most of these corporations are simply searching for a high-risk gamble with a technological flavor, not for a long-term, sustained effort with a clear plan. Meanwhile, the two or three U.S. ceramics companies are being wasted as a technology resource: one is being slowly disaggregated and sold off. A sad story.

V

What does all this tell us about U.S. industry's R&D management of the vital links between a basic research insight (the latter, in the ceramics story, was the Harwell work and Lange's understanding of its significance) and innovation (in ceramics, now coming from Japan)? How can U.S. companies avoid these pitfalls and win payoffs from their investment in R&D?

It is interesting that, although Peters and Waterman in their bestselling book, *In Search of Excellence*, offer relevant answers, the book deals practically nowhere with science. We would argue that the panicky, short-term attitudes of U.S. industrial managers suddenly wanting to enter the "opening" to ceramics is all too common. Used to believing they can run their business top-down, and make it profitable by manipulating short-term goals and activities, they can be lured to "rush" into inappropriate technology development as easily as they can be tempted into snapping up another acquisition.

The saddest part, from our particular viewpoint of concern for science and the profession of science, is that today's business leaders probably don't think they have to understand ceramics to get into the game. That is "just science" and not for nonscientists to understand. Perhaps they haven't had enough science courses in high school or college to dare to try to understand or want to risk being shown up in conversation with technical people. After all, there is a human factor: they are accustomed to dominating and they probably think to themselves, "Isn't science different, lofty, remote, something for the eggheads to do with their big accelerators?" In short, the value system of the postwar science elite seems to have spread to industry managers.

How to cure it? Peters and Waterman offer several fascinating clues. Their survey did include some "excellent" high-tech firms: Hewlett-Packard, IBM, Texas Instruments, and 3M. They also looked intensively at Digital Equipment, General Electric, Lockheed, TRW, and others.[20]

Now the "excellent" companies have few top managers. These allow "product champions" to prosper — even though these are often nonconformists and fanatical about their causes — because they command loyalty and get things done. These companies value experimentation over loads of analysis by committees before a product is even tested. All allow free flow among departments and encourage the kind of mixing we saw at Bell Laboratories.

3M has continuously innovated in a wide variety of products from Scotch tape to abrasive grain for grinding wheels. It is described as "so intent on innovation that its essential atmosphere seems not like that of a large corporation but rather a loose network of laboratories and cubbyholes populated by inventors and dauntless entrepreneurs who let their imaginations fly off in all directions." 3M does not keep its people on a tight rein, but encourages practical risk-taking: it tolerates the fact that this policy brings mistakes as well as successes.

Digital Equipment Corporation makes a point of moving fast to figure things out and then try them. One executive was quoted as saying, "When we've got a big problem here, we grab ten senior guys and stick them in a room for a week. They come up with an answer and implement them." Instead of allowing 250 engineers and marketers to work on a new product in isolation for 15 months, Peters and Waterman said "they form bands of 5 to 25 and test ideas out on a customer, often with inexpensive prototypes, within a matter of weeks." Also, Peters and Waterman were told that the innovativeness of a group in one company goes down as soon as that group has more than seven people.

Hewlett-Packard, for example, makes great effort to avoid the stultification that comes with size. Peters and Waterman found they could not walk around that company's facilities in Palo Alto without seeing "lots of people sitting together in rooms, working on problems." "Any one of these ad hoc meetings is likely to include people from R&D, manufacturing, engineering, marketing and sales." Peters and Waterman decided that Hewlett-Packard and 3M have developed a "technology of keeping in touch."

This emphasis on informality, communication, and local zeal was key to IBM's innovativeness. No major IBM product innovation for 25 years, they write, has come from the formal system of the company. The company's model 360 computer, a market triumph, had an extremely informal development process inside the company. Its topsy-turvy history was one reason for its success. To us, the characteristics that have kept giants like IBM or Texas Instruments creative and innovative sound very much like the characteristics of small R&D firms, which are well established as the greatest source of innovation in the country.

All the innovative companies, big and small, avoid overrational planning, big formal networks for clearances, and the like. But these are the exceptions rather than the rule in U.S. business today. Peters and Waterman write:

The dominant culture in most big companies demands punishment for a mistake, no matter how useful, small, invisible . . . This is especially ironic because the most noble ancestor of today's business rationality was called *scientific* management. Experimentation is the fundamental tool of science; if we experiment successfully, by definition we will make many mistakes. But overly rational businessmen are in pretty good company here, because even science doesn't own up to its messy road to progress.[21]

In *Zen and the Art of Motorcycle Maintenance*, Robert Persig describes the "spectator" attitude towards his "machine"—his motorcycle—that applies equally well to the management of too many U.S. companies. These have become mere "spectators" of the technology they use, an attitude which could be fatal economically. Persig writes,

While at work I was thinking about this lack of care in the digital computer manuals I was editing . . . They were full of errors, ambiguities, omissions and information so completely screwed up you had to read them six times to make any sense out of them. But what struck me for the first time was the agreement of these manuals with the spectator attitude I had seen in the shop. These were spectator manuals . . . Implicit in every line is the idea that, "Here is the machine, isolated in time and space from everything else in the universe. It has no relationship to you, you have no relationship to it, other than to turn certain switches, maintain certain voltage levels, check for error conditions" and so on. The mechanics in their attitude towards the machine were really taking no different attitude from the manual's toward the machine or from the attitude I had when I brought it there. We were all spectators. It then occurred to me, there *is* no manual that deals with the *real* business of motorcycle maintenance, the most important aspect of all. Caring about what you're doing is considered either unimportant or taken for granted.[22]

U.S. industry's problem is that executives and mid-level managers in marketing, finance, and even in engineering and research think of themselves as "spectators." Too many are seriously misinformed about the process of technological innovation and change. Too many think of an innovation as the schoolchild's version of Alexander Graham Bell's telephone or Thomas A. Edison's light bulb: a single bolt from the blue that revolutionizes an industry overnight. Many doubtless wish that some white-coated genius in their laboratories would invent today's equivalent of the light bulb. They ignore Edison's admonition that genius is 1 percent inspiration and 99 percent perspiration, and see no connection between themselves and the task of bringing "almost technology" to market.

Yet clearly, U.S. industry will need to advance technologically in order to survive. Engineers will have to get back down on the production line and in the workshops, instead of playing in the company's remote, antiseptic laboratory. Union leaders will have to understand technology so they can see that a different production technique could be good in the long run, even if it lays off workers now. (The impact of the process metallurgy we noted earlier on unionized steel plants which will have to be rebuilt is one example.) Accountants and executives are going to have to see R&D as "a producer of tomorrow's wealth," not as "a cost center," as Peter Drucker wrote. Salespeople will have to understand not only the product but the technology behind it, and how that technology is evolving and how the next product will be better. The CEOs now busy acquiring unrelated businesses will have to recognize the real cost of their habit.

Management, in short, will have to change — just as we argue that the profession of science will have to change in order for them to meet halfway on the mutual turf of technology.

NOTES

[1] Peter F. Drucker, "Science and Industry, Challenges of Antagonistic Interdependence," *Science* 204 (25 May 1979), p. 808.

[2] Barnaby J. Feder, "The Research Aid in the New Tax Law," *New York Times* (29 Sept. 1981), pp. D1 and D11.

[3] *Science Indicators 1982* (Washington, D.C., National Science Board, 1983), pp. 92, 93.

[4] Ted G. Berlincourt, Harold Weinstock, and Francis Narin, "Performer Affiliations and Funding Sources for Research Reported in Physi-

cal Review Letters and Applied Physics Letters: Historical Trends and Implications." Available through the Office of Naval Research. Summaries appeared in *Physics Today* (November 1982), p. 9ff.

[5] Jean Mayer, "Decline in Industrial Engineering," *Science* 218 (10 December 1982), p. 1073.

[6] See Charles G. Burck, "A Group Profile of the Fortune 500 Executive," *Fortune* 93 (May 1976), pp. 172–77, 308, 311–12. The chemical sector has remained strong technically, and it has a relatively high proportion of top managers with chemistry backgrounds. See William J. Storck, "More Top Managers Have Technical Backgrounds," *Chemical and Engineering News* (6 December 1982), p. 9ff.

[7] Thomas J. Peters and Robert H. Waterman, Jr., *In Search of Excellence, Lessons from America's Best-Run Companies* (New York: Harper & Row, 1982).

[8] Chalmers W. Sherwin and Raymond S. Isenson, "Project Hindsight: A Defense Department Study of the Utility of Research," *Science* 156 (22 June 1967), p. 1571ff.

[9] TRACES is published at Illinois Institute of Technology Research Institute, "Technology in Retrospect and Critical Events in Science," prepared for the National Science Foundation under Contract NSF-C535, 1968, 118 pp. The sequel is Batelle-Columbus Laboratories, "Science, Technology and Innovation," prepared for the National Science Foundation under Contract NSF C-667, Columbus, Ohio, 1973, 33 pp.

Both are cited in Richard Kremer and Mary Ellen Mogee, "Two Decades of Research on Innovation: Selected Studies of Current Relevance," in *Special Study on Economic Change*, vol. 3, *Research and Innovation, Developing a Dynamic Nation*, Joint Economic Committee of the Congress, 29 December 1980, pp. 163–165.

[10] Richard R. Nelson (ed.), *Government and Technical Progress: A Cross-Industry Analysis* (New York: Pergamon Press, 1982), p. 3.

[11] This history is based on Prescott C. Mabon, *Mission: Communications, The Story of Bell Laboratories* (Bell Telephone Laboratories, Inc., 1975), pp. 152, 153. Interviews with Bell Laboratories officials.

[12] Ibid., p. 158.

[13] Richard C. Levin, "The Semiconductor Industry," in Nelson, *op. cit.*, pp. 40–43, 47–57.

[14] Nelson, *op. cit.*, pp. 58–75.

[15] Mabon, *op. cit.*, p. 163.

[16] Vannevar Bush, *Science—The Endless Frontier* (Washington, D.C.: National Science Foundation, 1960), NSF 60-40, pp. 22, 10.

[17] Discussion based on R. E. Evenson, "Agriculture," in Nelson, *op. cit.*, pp. 233–282.

[18] A recent federal critique of the system is "Science for Agriculture," report of a workshop on Critical Issues in American Agricultural Research, jointly sponsored by the Rockefeller Foundation and the Office of Science and Technology Policy, Executive Office of the President, 13–16 June 1982, Winrock International Conference Center, Morrilton, Arkansas.

[19] The history and rationale for this tradition, and Keyworth's office's endorsement of it, appears in *Aeronautical Research and Technology Policy* (Washington, D.C., Office of Science and Technology Policy, 1982).

[20] Peters and Waterman, *op. cit.*, pp. 14–16, 94, 104–140 passim.

[21] *Ibid.*, p. 48.

[22] Robert Persig, *Zen and the Art of Motorcycle Maintenance* (New York: Morrow, 1974), pp. 34–35. Quoted in Peters and Waterman, *op. cit.*, pp. 37–38.

4
The Human Factor

W<small>E ARE CONCERNED</small> with the inner workings of the science profession and its relation to society and the economy, now and in future. What goals do scientists set for their profession? What do they teach students are "good" and "bad" professional activities? What rituals do they hold most dear? Are the profession's internal workings helping or hurting it and the nation adapt to technological, economic, and social change?

It is tempting to think that professions may follow some law of natural selection, in which a species' once-useful features — like plumage, rituals, or even protuberances such as the 12-foot-wide horns of the great Irish elk — become disadvantages when its environment changes.[1] When the grassy, open country of Ireland changed to tundra, the Irish elk suffered; when forests sprouted, the antlers tangled, causing the magnificent deer's demise. The modern equivalent of these ancient Irish forests may be springing up around some of the postwar exuberances of U.S. science.

This chapter discusses some of the profession's rituals, which may have been useful and necessary to the followers of Vannevar Bush, who sought to assure the best high science in the United States after the professional wrenchings of World War II. Administrative encumbrances, peer review of proposals, and the growth in journals to accommodate the rising numbers of scientists — these trappings were probably proper in their day. But now that the profession is so big and so complex, they often hinder free-flowing creative work — let alone the synergistic relationship between engineering, development, applied science, and purposive basic research we think necessary today.

The chapter also takes up what professors teach their students are "good" and "bad" professional activities. Obviously, the most important thing young scientists should be taught is to stick to the lab day and night, to get to the cutting edge of the field as fast as possible, and to join professional societies and commute to meetings. But it is *not* good that they are not encouraged to help with science education in the schools and are discouraged from even teaching freshmen. Scientists do undertake some public service: it is respectable and important that they take time away from research to study nuclear winter or arms control or the environment. It is also professionally respectable to spend time in Washington, testifying about the laser and fission and polio to get the next research budget appropriated. But it has not been respectable for the scientist to become involved with school committees, high school science teachers, the education researchers — most of whom are viewed as second-raters by the basic-research-is-best crowd.

I

A standard defense of U.S. academic science is that the university science system gives excellent training to graduate students and postdocs embarking on their careers. But an increasing number of young U.S. scientists are deciding *not* to go to graduate school in the "hard" (or physical) sciences. There has been a decline in the number of bachelors of engineering who go on to graduate school. The number of M.D.s who go on to get their Ph.D.s has been declining, too. So while some leaders brag about our fine university system, young Americans are voting otherwise with their feet.

Figure 10 shows the decline in the number of U.S. citizens obtaining Ph.D.s in the "hard" sciences and engineering. The trends

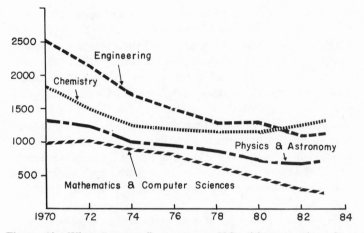

Figure 10 What "message" are young U.S. citizens getting about science? Overall, in the hard sciences, the numbers of U.S. citizens earning the Ph.D. degree has been declining, as the figure shows. Meanwhile, overall Ph.D. enrollments have been increasing slightly, and a larger percentage have been foreign students. (SOURCE: National Research Council, Office of Scientific and Engineering Personnel, Doctorate Records File.)

are different for the different fields. Nonetheless, the curves go downward, even in fields where total graduate enrollments are increasing as a result of the influx of foreign graduate students. There is some debate about the foreign students and their impact on the campus and the scientific work force,[2] but less attention is being paid to the alarming decline of U.S. citizens seeking advanced training in the physical sciences. Although one factor discouraging them is the lack of openings at the university for postdocs and young professors, nonetheless, David Shirley, Director of the Lawrence Berkeley Laboratory, told an audience in 1982, "I think we are sending our young people the wrong message about science."

Clearly, if bright young Americans continue to be "turned off" university research, the consequences will be serious for the nation. The declining number of M.D.s going into academic medicine is already a cause of concern.[3] Many, including Lewis

Thomas, Chancellor of Memorial Sloan-Kettering Cancer Center in New York, say that as a result, there may be fewer advances comparable to those which came from the postwar coupling of university research and clinical practice, through the M.D.–Ph.D. system. Finally, fewer and fewer doctorate holders in the sciences and engineering plan to work in universities, while a rising number are planning to work in industry.

Many factors lie behind this trend, among them the pressure young people feel to start earning a living as soon as possible. But Thomas adds that young M.D.s are turned off by the older generation: "The young are looking at us, and we seem to them to be an anxious and unhappy bunch of people," he said.

> Ten years ago research used to be fun, a very great pleasure and an honor. Now it's not. The amount of paperwork is an order of magnitude more tedious. The [paperwork] material is too detailed. . . . [We're] all worried about grant renewals or whether there is a job ahead for our students.[4]

Now, science has always been hard work. Great discoveries and many lesser ones have been made by scientists who slept in their laboratories, or worked feverishly for days and months. Hard, even obsessive, work is one of the attractions of science, one of its intellectual pleasures, one reason it should draw strong, aggressively creative people.

The complaint today is that the U.S. research system is quenching out such enthusiasm. It often prevents scientists from working in a sustained, intense way. It makes the daily business of science distracting and tedious. Philip Abelson, Editor of *Science*, summarizes the general perception of malaise:

> During the past 2 months I have had casual conversations with about 20 professors from widely scattered universities. If their attitudes are an indication of the spirit on campus, the long-term future of science in America is in jeopardy. Not one of the 20 conveyed the impression that life is great, science is fun, and that academic research is the best possible of all activities. Rather the majority were gloomy — some were bitter.[5]

In the past 10 or 15 years, conditions have changed from the 1950s and early 1960s. Then the system was smaller, more informal, and more stable. Then it more nearly matched the idea expressed, among other places, in *Science—The Endless Frontier*:

> Scientific progress on a broad front results from the free play of free intellects, working on subjects of their own choice, in the manner dictated by their curiosity for exploration of the unknown. Freedom of inquiry must be preserved under any plan for government support.[6]

These words may have a bitter ring to today's practicing scientists and graduate students. Government support today does not bring with it freedom in Bush's sense. Often, it brings the opposite. Bush's ideal of freedom persists in some places—possibly at Oxford or Cambridge in Great Britain, where scientists have time to engage in "the free play of free intellects" and where they are hardly rich, but they are not financially insecure either. U.S. scientists now mainly work in large research mills full of "anxious and unhappy" people. Often unrealistically short-term projects live or die at the whims of anonymous peer reviewers and government bureaus. Many U.S. scientists have simply lost control over what they do, and when and how they do it. Small wonder, then, that private industry is looking so attractive to young and old alike. The unprecedented federal funds spent on science in recent years have brought, alas, unprecedented insecurity.

II

Three main rituals stand between the practicing scientist and his overarching need to do the most creative work possible. One is the amount of time spent *not* doing research or teaching but doing petty tasks. Second is the requirement that even short-term awards of federal funds be peer-reviewed beforehand, a system articulated throughout the federal administration of science and thoroughly vestigial. Third is the excessive publication of scientific papers, a requirement that scientists follow slavishly to acquire professional status but one that makes knowledge difficult to synthesize and increasingly dated in an era of expanding electronic data communications.

Today, many of the daily chores of science have nothing to do with doing experiments, thinking about theories, or "the free play of free intellects." The selection of experiments is dictated as much by where the money is and what will please peer reviewers as it is by curiosity or judgment as to what is important science. The scientific work itself is too often the least strenuous part; instead, the strain and excitement go into getting the next grant and into worrying about personnel. This also takes a heavy toll on graduate students and postdocs who flutter insecurely among projects like atoms in Brownian motion.

The statistics bear this out. Whereas the number of full-time equivalent workers in academic research and development (R&D) grew at 4 percent per year from 1973 to 1978, since then it has been a different story. The latest *Science Indicators* report measuring the overall "health" of science reported that this increase slowed to a crawl of only 1 percent each year from 1978 to 1981. In other words, the numbers of hours faculty reported doing research, as opposed to teaching or administrative chores, increased only a tiny amount. Said *Science Indicators*: "This decline in growth has been attributed to the increased utilization of graduate research assistants who may be offsetting full-time professional staff in academic R&D activities."[7] What, we ask, are these busy faculty doing while their graduate students work for them in the laboratory?

Moreover, the number of volumes added to university libraries has been decreasing, meaning that less of the growing body of new knowledge is getting into the hands of teachers and students. The state of scientific instrumentation on campuses is poor, although the science community has launched a successful lobbying effort in Washington to turn this around. Still, *Science Indicators* reported that more than 25 percent of university instrumentation is more than 10 years old. When the Department of Defense arranged to distribute some $30 million for university instrumentation, it was flooded with requests for instruments totaling $670 million![8] The field of mathematics, whose sister field of computer science has been glamorous for a decade or more, turns out to be doing poorly. It suffers from declining enrollment, old equipment, and even less secretarial help than other science departments. Small wonder that in several fields the professors who are role models for young scientists are "an anxious and unhappy bunch."

Meanwhile, both senior and junior academic scientists are locked in deadly competition for grant awards. Competition in moderate doses is one of the healthy features of the U.S. science system, as we shall see in Chapter 5, but at present levels it seems out of control. Competition encourages a given bit of science to be broken down into the greatest number of publishable parts, so that each participant can get the most professional credit. Yet, this fragments knowledge, makes it harder to understand, and thwarts synthesis.

The procedures of the scientific profession have become partial obstacles to doing good science even though it is the job of a profession *not* to put obstacles between its practitioners and their goals. What if doctors were allowed to see their patients only after circulating a 100-page plan for how they will treat them? In medicine, once doctors are certified to practice, they are trusted to go about their duties to the best of their abilities. This is not the case with science.

Our science system borders on presuming that the best environment for science is some kind of Darwinian jungle where only the fittest survive. Unfortunately, too many of the "anxious and unhappy bunch" feel like survivors, crawling out of a jungle. What kind of people survive in it? People who are adept at juggling administrative and scientific tasks, who don't mind constant travels on business (not science), and who are good office workers. People who can keep students by remembering, for example, that these three aren't getting paid this month and find funds—legally or nearly so—for them to eat until the next grant begins. Who does not survive? The scientist who is poor at these things, who is obsessive and lost in his or her work, who can't stand filling out forms or meeting quarterly deadlines or complying with laboratory animal welfare regulations. In short, the kind of person who

The need to free scientists from administrative and regulatory constraints. (SOURCE: Nalimov, p. 91.)

stays up all night in the laboratory — and forgets about making the morning plane to the study section meeting. The sort of person who doesn't care what colleagues think because they're a bunch of so-so's anyway. In other words, the kind of scientist who, throughout history, has made dazzling contributions to knowledge.

The second ritual that gets in the way of good science is peer review. Contrary to popular wisdom, there *are* good alternatives to it. The term "peer review" in the context of science policy has acquired a deep symbolism within the science community. It is repeated like a mantra or used as a talisman to shield any activity, put it above reproach, so to speak. Future historians of science will perhaps delve into how all this occurred in 40 short years.

Many of those we interviewed recalled fondly how peer review was handled in the "good old days" by the Office of Naval Research (ONR). Then, a Navy program manager, himself an active participant in the research field he monitored, upon receiving a brief plan of work from a scientist, would call up two or three persons whose views he respected, ask their opinion, and decide whether or not to fund it. Two fundamental features of ONR's system distinguish it from the way peer review works today. First, note the role of the research manager in making the decision. Even today, the ONR permits its staff to make grant awards without relying on peer reviews, unlike most federal science agencies. In the ONR system, then, *someone takes responsibility* for making choices, and uses the peers only as advisors.

Another difference is that in the late 1940s and 1950s science was smaller. The two or three people who served as reviewers might not work in the exact subfield of the work proposed. This kind of reviewing then asked what good the work would be to other specialties. And, the ONR officer probably was asking what the work would do for the Navy. Thus, the old ONR system often enabled the work to be evaluated from fresh perspectives. (Note that both these characteristics — research managers who make decisions and take responsibility for them and informal reviews by those in and outside of one's field — were characteristic of the Bell Laboratories' management of research described in the previous chapter.)

Nobel laureate Rosalyn Yalow, physicist Richard Muller (winner of NSF's Waterman prize), and one of us have separately criticized the peer review system.[9] The complaints are:

- The system wastes a great deal of the time of talented people who are in short supply.
- We have no definition of what constitutes the best science.
- We have no good, consistent definition of what constitutes a peer.

- Reviewers often have conflicts of interest, despite precautions.
- Science based on careful proposals worked out in advance ignores the vital role of chance and serendipity.
- It saps the morale of the community, and tempts its members into soft cheating.
- It puts a premium on groupthink and straitjacketing of ideas.

Moreover, as the body of scientific knowledge has grown, and with it specialization, peer review has a stultifying effect rather than a refreshing one. "Peers" have come be defined more and more narrowly, as those who work in the *exact* subspecialty in which the proposal falls. Paradoxically, work in a fast-breaking field or one in which the nation is weakest, yet which may be critical nationally, may have a hard time getting started because it has no constituency of peers. Although there are efforts to change this trend, most peer review groups have become specialized cells. Outsiders from even other subspecialties are excluded as unqualified. A seminal study by Cole, Cole, and Simon found that chance was a significant factor in determining whether or not a peer-reviewed proposal was funded. Of 150 proposals submitted to the NSF and decided upon by a first round of peer review, as many as 30 percent had their verdicts changed by a second round.[10]

One could whimsically compare science's definition of judgment by one's peers with that used in English and American law. Although the two peer systems serve very different purposes (the law uses it to judge an accused's deviation from accepted norms, whereas, at best, science uses it to discover and ratify new norms), they are easily blurred. When we try an accused bank robber through a jury of his peers, we do not insist that the members of the jury belong in his subspecialty, be it safe-cracking, money-laundering, or beating old ladies. Nor do we choose juries mostly of criminals, with one law-abiding citizen added just for spice. If the courts were to use the science system's de facto definition of "peer," bank robbers would be judged only by bank robbers and axe murderers only by axe murderers. These juries might even acquit a guilty party and commend him for his specialized technical accomplishments! The parody is not altogether facetious: perhaps similar things have happened in science!

The old edifice may finally be starting to crumble, as criticism has mounted. Back in the 1960s Congressman George Miller, Chairman of the House Science and Technology Committee, introduced a bill that would fund science on a formula basis. According to Congressman Emilio Q. Daddario, the academic community's resistance killed the bill. Yet some sort of formula system seems inevitable. One of us has developed such a formula which retains a peer review feature.[11] It is based on the productivity of the individual scientist over previous years. Productivity is measured by all the products of the scientist, many of which are peer-reviewed: published papers, graduated M.S. and Ph.D. students, research support from industry (a meaningful form of review, we argue), and support from federal mission agencies.

An alternative is a hybrid system of funding used in Great Britain and the Soviet Union. One part is a block grant to a group or laboratory or department, and the other part is based on simple proposals which permit reviewers mainly to evaluate the applicant's track record. An important change would be to follow Weinberg's notion and have scientists from neighboring disciplines sit in judgment on an entire subfield, to see how it is doing and where it should go. Blocks of money could be awarded, say, for cell membrane studies by the NIH, which the cell membrane people would decide, by formula or consensus, how to spend. Now, the peer system pits specialists in the same field in continuous competition. It prevents the consensus-building needed for them to decide among themselves how to use limited funds. Clearly, a better balance between consensus and competition can be achieved.

However, in September 1984, the NSF acquired its first director from industry: this is Erich Bloch, formerly Vice President of Technical Personnel Development at IBM. Likewise, the new chairman of the National Science Board is from industry: Roland Schmitt, formerly Senior Vice President for Corporate Research and Development of General Electric. These appointees reflect the current administration's interest in experimenting with traditional research administration. And Bloch and Schmitt may be personally more disposed to experiment than their predecessors. Another promising development is the appointment of a panel by the President's science adviser, George A. Keyworth II, headed by David Packard to study alternative ways to fund science. It may be that these political appointees will have the courage to reform science funding – courage the profession so far has been reluctant to show.

A final ritual is publication, which is supposed to be the principal way by which scientists communicate findings and replicate the findings of others. Nothing could be more desirable than to publish findings as fully and openly as possible. But today's publication serves other purposes as well. Mostly certification. Each publication lengthens a scientist's publications list, and the longer the list, the more likely he or she will be awarded grants.

Earlier, the editors of scientific journals *really* ran them – they even put their names on journals such as *Liebig's Annalen der Pharmacie*, published in the nineteenth century by German chemist Justus von Liebig. Even after 1945 in Europe, crusty and magisterial editors reigned over journals, deciding what to accept, arguing *with* authors, *directly*, making judgments. U.S. editors did too. Martin Buerger of M.I.T. presided thus over the *Zeitschrift fur Kristallographie;* Adolf Pabst of the University of California at Berkeley ran the *American Mineralogist.*

Gradually, the informal advice such editors sought from colleagues became codified into a system of anonymous refereeing, or peer-reviewing. This was to guarantee quality in an era of specialization. But in practice, as John Ziman[12] and Derek deSolla Price have pointed out, it reaffirms the group's preconceived notions of what aspect of science is important. Nonetheless, this process for evaluating the worth of research *after* it is done was taken over by government science agencies, to evaluate research *before* it is done. Now the review systems for journal submissions and for grant proposals mirror each other and sometimes compete as to which can be the most formal. With the decline of the editors' roles, the responsibility for whether a paper is published now rests all too easily with anonymous reviewers. Several journal editors we know even enjoy sneaking around the review process and publishing papers their reviewers don't like!

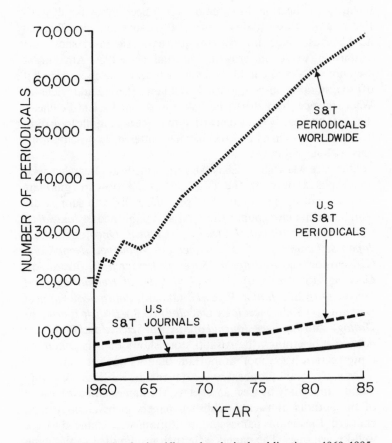

Figure 11 Growth of scientific and technical publications, 1960–1985. Although the philosophical and professional principles of scientific publication have not changed since the postwar system was established in the 1950s, the number and character of scientific publications has changed dramatically since 1960. (SOURCE: Donald W. King, Dennis D. McDonald, Nancy K. Roderer, King Research Inc., "The Journal in Scientific Communication: The Roles of Authors, Publishers, Libraries and Readers in a Vital System," May 1979, for National Science Foundation, Figure 9, p. 32.)

Several structural things have perverted the original aim of scientific publication. First, even though peer review is still justified as a means of quality control, any paper can get published now because there are so many journals. Figure 11 shows the astonishing worldwide growth of journals since 1960. Anything — even hoaxes — can be published *some*where: the trick is to send it off to a suitably obscure journal. William J. Broad and Nicholas Wade, science journalists who have investigated scientific cheating, note how easily some con artists manage to compile long publications lists, even of articles they had pilfered, in obscure journals without being caught.

One case was that of Elias Alsabti, a medical researcher who was exposed only by the diligence of an obscure graduate student — not by the hundreds of peer reviewers who supposedly read his work before publication. Alsabti published in *Journal of Cancer Research and Journal of Clinical Oncology* (U.S.), *Japanese Journal of Experimental Medicine*, *Neoplasma* (Czechoslovakia), *European Surgical Research* (Switzerland), *Oncology* (Switzerland), *Journal of Clinical Hematology and Oncology* (U.S.), *Tumor Research* (Japan), *Journal of Surgical Oncology* (U.S.), *Gynecologic Oncology* (U.S.), *British Journal of Urology*, and *Japanese Journal of Medical Science and Biology*.[13] Among other things, the Alsabti story shows that the *length* of a publication list is more important than its quality.

As with a grant proposal review, journal review does not assure quality. In a study by Ceci and Peters, the names and affiliations of the authors of twelve published papers in psychology were changed. Prestigious names and institutions were changed to less well-known ones. The papers were then resubmitted to the same set of journals that had already published them. Not only did the peer reviewers selected by these journals fail to detect the prior publication of nine of the twelve papers they were reviewing, but, of the nine, they rejected eight as unsuitable for publication![14]

The Ceci and Peters study became a major flap. Initially, journal editors and others pressured Ceci and Peters not to publish their study. Only after the press got word of this imminent censorship, did one journal, *Behavioral and Brain Science*, publish it. Its editor, to his credit, followed up with fifty-six other papers and commentaries on the subject of peer review. This issue offers insights into the human factors involved in scientific publishing.[15]

III

Finally, professions also teach their members some form of public service. Science has a long and honorable tradition in this regard, the best known causes since 1945 having been control of atomic energy and arms control. But some forms of public service are more professionally respectable than others. Without disputing the motives of those scientists who commute to Washington to advise the government and to erudite private and foreign conferences on these matters, we would guess that most public-spirited members of the profession have probably not given much thought to running for their town's local school board.

Perhaps this is, indirectly, the result of the decline of the cities. A professor might run for the school committee in an elm-shaded rural town, where his or her peers would be on it too. But many of our major universities are in large cities; beyond their walls lie often a wasteland of buildings, underutilized people, and poor city services, including the schools.

Nonetheless, the schools house a sizable portion of the next generation of technicians, accountants, lawyers, small businessmen, and, of course, future scientists and engineers. For 3 years now, the poor state of U.S. primary and secondary education has been a national scandal, in particular, the poor state of teaching of science and mathematics.[16] The educational community has been trying to figure out for itself how to teach the schoolchildren better. The business community is alarmed, for the specter of employees who are so poorly educated that they cannot do simple tasks well bodes ill for business. The military, it is said, issues comic books to servicemen to instruct them to operate things like the modern Sherman tank. The country, in short, has discovered that its people need to know science and math.

What will be the science profession's role in solving the problem? Remedying it and catching up to the Soviet and Japanese educational systems will be difficult. Our pluralistic educational system prevents swift, top-down curriculum reform; federal dollars to education, like federal dollars to applied science and development, are the subject of intense negotiation with powerful lobbies. For example, suggestions to create "master teachers" — to reward some teachers who happen to be gifted at their craft with recognition and more pay — have been resisted by teachers' groups as likely to cause resentment. While excellence in education may be a clear goal, the process of achieving it is thoroughly muddy.

As this is written, the President has just signed a law that will give the NSF $50 million for teacher training institutes and other aids to math and science education. The bill also gives the Department of Education approximately $200 million, which will flow to states to improve curriculum, upgrade the quality and supply of teachers, and help underprivileged children, including in science and math. (The bill also directs the NSF to support university–industry partnerships, but this part has not been funded.)

The President is playing the issue too. Last year, he upstaged Congress' momentum by holding a White House conference honoring math and science teachers; recently, he announced that a teacher would be the first member of the public to go into space. But his curbs on domestic spending nix any chance of a major federal remedial program. The education lobby, for example, would like $3 billion a year to cure the problem.

The science community could greatly improve the quality of math and science education in the nation's schools, but it may well opt out of this responsibility. For years, the profession has been concerned with education only in the narrowest sense: the finding and training of the next crop of graduate students.

These attitudes have been mirrored in the institutional reluctance of the NSF, which has a mandate in its enabling legislation to "develop and encourage the pursuit of a national policy for the promotion of basic research and education in the sciences," to become the champion of undergraduate and precollege science teaching. Figure 12 shows the percentage of the NSF's budget since 1952 that has gone to science education, including curriculum and materials development, institutes for science teachers, and fellowships for young scientists. It shows the spurt in interest that followed Sputnik, when the teachers' institutes were ex-

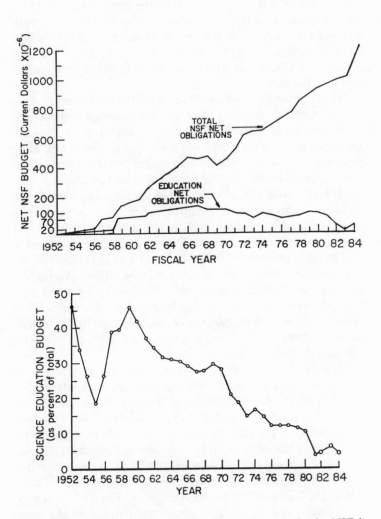

Figure 12 The decline in science education's fortunes in the NSF is highlighted by comparing the steady growth of NSF's total budget (*top*) with the dramatic decline in the percentage allotted to science education (*bottom*). (SOURCE: National Science Foundation.)

panded and NSF money went to fund the development of up-to-date and innovative course materials in physics, chemistry, biology and mathematics. It also shows science education's decline, from 46 percent to approximately 1.5 percent of NSF's budget through 1983. Now, Congress is literally forcing the education role down NSF's throat.

It has repeatedly voted more money for the NSF to improve the state of math and science education than the Reagan administration wants or than the NSF appears willing to spend. The administration first tried to zero out science education at NSF completely; but when the political groundswell for some government action loomed in 1983, it grudgingly asked for $39 million for fiscal 1984. In fiscal 1983, Congress had appropriated $30 million, or almost twice the administration's request; in fiscal 1984, it upped the administration's ante to $75 million. Meanwhile, the NSF had been unable to spend $14 of the $30 million appropriated in 1983, so for fiscal 1984 it had a total of $89 million available, of which it managed to dispense only $58 million. And all this at the height of a supposed national "crisis" over science and math illiteracy in the nation! As we have been saying, some parts of our postwar science system don't take the "national" view in their anxiety to preserve long-standing customs and rituals that serve the special needs of university science.

Historically, the NSF has been reluctant to get into general public science education, according to its historian, J. Merton England. There were several reasons, some better founded than others. One reason was that the U.S. school system was enormous compared with the NSF, so it could not "do something" in the field without distorting the rest of the agency. Another reason was the political power of the Office of Education. A third, less commendable reason was that the NSF and its university science clientele might "demean" themselves (England's words).[17] In the debates that followed Sputnik, about what it should do about science education, the NSF nearly always chose to train a small number of very high quality scientists over "quantity" production of scientifically knowledgeable people. Meanwhile, both the Soviet Union and Japan have chosen to train huge numbers of students in science and engineering, and required a knowledge of science in its general populace. The result of these choices is coming home to roost today.

Individuals in the profession may feel outright disdain for the problem of educating the general student population about science. We collected many stories in our interviews of professors being told by their department heads not to "waste" their time teaching undergraduate courses. Except for the monetary incentive of writing a best-selling undergraduate textbook (few of which succeed), they have no immediate motive to organize to improve courses for nonscientists.

Indeed, one reason for the uninspiring rote methods, the unimaginative use of new technology, the out-of-date materials in science teaching in U.S. schools is that this aloofness is shared by educators, also. They too regard science as remote and specialized, a burden to impose on teachers and students as little as possible. Science teaching has thus suffered from *both* the scientists' and educators' lack of interest. It is high time the science profession opened the door of its university laboratory, marched down to school in the (usually poor) neighborhoods nearby, squatted in a pint-sized chair, set up a piece of simple equipment as a teaching tool, and let the children crowd around.

The scientific profession, to call itself a profession, must reassume a role in general scientific education. Already there are some well-intentioned attempts to reach out to local students, particularly to high school students already interested in science. Fermilab in Chicago, for example, holds Saturday morning physics workshops for local high school students. Caltech has a similar program. But these are token efforts, undertaken at relatively little cost. And bright, motivated high school students are, after all, a self-selected group. University professors may be more willing to give time to them because they see them as future grist for their graduate student mill.

These token efforts do not address the key question, which is whether U.S. science will participate vigorously in the effort to educate the public generally about science and engineering. Bush's report, *Science—The Endless Frontier*, anticipated this problem. One of the committees, chaired by Henry Allen Moe of the Guggenheim Foundation, wrote:

. . . we are not interested in setting up an elect. We think it much the best plan, in this constitutional Republic, that opportunity be held out to all kinds and conditions of men whereby they can better themselves. This is the American way. . . . [18]

And it quoted a statement made at Oxford that is a plea for general education that truly incorporates science into it, instead of treating science as something remote and separate from the general culture:

We live in a world in which science lies at the very roots of community, and a mastery of scientific thinking grows more and more indispensable for the successful practice of the arts of life. The culture of the modern age, if it is to have meaning, must be deeply imbued with scientific ways of thought. It must absorb science, without forsaking what is of value in the older ways. . . .

It is a question, not of substituting a scientific culture for that which has gone before, but of reaching a wider appreciation in which the sciences in their modern development fall into their due place. [19]

These goals are still not attained and are just as relevant today.

NOTES

[1] Stephen Jay Gould, *Ever Since Darwin* (New York: W. W. Norton, 1977), pp. 79, 81, 90.

[2] Crauford D. Goodwin and Michael Nacht, "Absence of Decision, Foreign Students in American Colleges and Universities, A Report on Policy Formation and the Lack Thereof" (New York: Institute of International Education, 1983).

[3] T. L. Bickel et al., "The Role of M.D.-Ph.D. Training in Increasing the Supply of Physician-Scientists," *New England Journal of Medicine* 304 (21 May 1981), pp. 1265–1268.

[4] Lewis Thomas interview with author Shapley. Notes.

[5] Philip Abelson, "Problems of Science Faculties," *Science*, 204 (1979), p. 133.

[6] Vannevar Bush, *Science—The Endless Frontier* (Washington, D.C.:

National Science Foundation) NSF 45–60, p. 12.

[7] *Science Indicators 1982*, National Science Board, Washington, D.C., 1983, p. 131.

[8] *Science Indicators 1982, op. cit.*, pp. 118, 133. Deborah Shapley, "US University Re-equipment," *Nature*, Vol. 301, p. 207.

[9] Rosalyn S. Yalow, "Is Subterfuge Consistent With Good Science," *Bulletin of Science Technology and Society*, 2 (1982), p. 401; Richard Muller, "Innovation and Science Funding," *Science*, 209 (22 August 1980), pp. 880–883; Rustum Roy, "Peer Review of Proposals – Rationale, Practice and Performance," *Bulletin of Science Technology and Society*, 2 (1982), p. 405.

[10] Stephen Cole, Jonathan R. Cole, and Gary A. Simon, "Chance and Consensus in Peer Review," *Science* 214 (20 November 1981), p. 881. A comprehensive discussion is Howard J. Sanders, "Peer Review, How Well Is It Working?," *Chemical and Engineering News* (15 March 1982), pp. 32ff.

[11] Roy formula appears in Sanders, *op. cit.*, and *Science* 211 (21 March 1981), p. 1377, and *Science* 212 (19 June 1981), p. 1338.

[12] John M. Ziman, *Reliable Knowledge: An Exploration of the Grounds for Belief in Science* (New York: Cambridge University Press, 1978). See also, Ziman, "Science: The New Model," *Bulletin of Science Technology and Society*, 1 (1981), p. 27.

[13] William Broad and Nicholas Wade, *Betrayers of the Truth* (New York: Simon and Shuster, 1982), p. 45.

[14] D. P. Peters and Stephen J. Ceci, "Peer-Review Practice of Psychological Journals: The Fate of Published Articles Submitted Again," *The Behavioral and Brain Science*, 5 (1982), pp. 187–196.

[15] S. Harnad, "Peer Commentary on Peer Review," *The Behavioral and Brain Science* 5 (1982), pp. 185–186 and followed by 56 authored comments, pp. 196–225.

[16] For documentation of the poor state of math and science education at the elementary, secondary, and undergraduate levels, see Hearings on HR 30, Education and Labor Committee, U.S. House of Representatives, 98th Congress, Jan. 1983.

[17] J. Merton England, *A Patron for Pure Science: The National Science Foundation's Formative Years, 1945–57* (Washington, D.C.: National Science Foundation, 1982), pp. 225, 226, Chap. 12.

[18] Bush, *op. cit.*, pp. 149, 150.

[19] *Ibid.* pp. 151, 152.

5

New International Factors

THE INTERNATIONAL environment in which U.S. science operates today is very different from that of the late 1940s and 1950s when the present arrangements for U.S. science were put in place. And just as U.S. industry no longer automatically dominates the international marketplace, U.S. science is no longer the undisputed leader internationally in every field. The new situation is as different from the old as night is from day or winter is from summer. More appropriately, it is like a new climatic epoch, in which a beast that adapted well to the earlier one must adapt yet again.

The new era is paradoxical, however. On the one hand, the climate for international collaboration in science—one of the profession's most important qualities—is warmer than ever. In virtually every major field U.S. scientists can point to significant work being done in Europe, the Soviet Union, Japan, Canada, or Israel that needs to be read closely, argued about, and replicated as much as does work done in the United States. On the other hand, the new era is chillier, for governments and businesses here and abroad will continue to try to squeeze economic value out of every bit of science to win the international high-tech sweepstakes. Already there are strong pressures to stop publication or communication of some scientific information for trade advantage or national security. The paradox of the new age, then, is that as communication and collaboration across national boundaries become more important, pressure to restrict them is growing, too. And, under our essay's plan to link basic and applied science more closely, the line between what to communicate and what to restrict will be hard to draw. Sophisticated judgments will have to be made by scientists and they will have to be very persuasive with their industrial sponsors or government security agencies. But then, we never said our plan would be easy.

One concern is that U.S. science, with a few marked exceptions (the outstanding one being high-energy physics), has not looked abroad to engage the international communication–collaboration process as rapidly and eagerly as it should. There are many reasons, such as economic and social pressures, and competition for tenure at home that deter postdoctoral students from spending the year in a European university that used to be *de rigueur.* There is the general inward-looking cast and preoccupation with professional rivalry discussed in Chapter 4. And citation analysis shows that the United States is one of the lowest in citing foreign work, overall (with exceptions in some fields, of course).[1]

It is possible—though difficult to prove, in any case—that the values of U.S. scientists have not kept pace with the times. Today, two-thirds of the world's scientific activity is done outside the United States. But although U.S. use of foreign scientific work has increased, we fear the U.S. science community has a not-invented-here syndrome and simply doesn't care enough about going to international meetings or reading foreign journals. (A well-known exception is the high-energy physicists, whose friendly competition in giant accelerator work dates back to the 1960s and who have been continuously transnationally peripatetic since the days of Einstein. Climatologists, geophysicists, and oceanographers are among the other exceptions.)

But all too often the attitude of government agencies has been to cut foreign travel, or not to compel project scientists to make a foreign trip when perhaps they should. U.S. scientists and grants administrators are not immune from our nation's isolationist tendencies. In science, this has been reinforced by decades of unquestioned U.S. preeminence. In plain language, we tend to be snobs.

The problem of the geographic distribution of science.
(SOURCE: Nalimov, p. 253.)

This chapter also discusses what U.S. science *policy* can learn from abroad. Every major western nation is experimenting — and we should be, too — with ways to structure science and technology to obtain both the highest quality science and the most economic value from the investment. In the new climatic epoch, we all face the same adapative problem. Western Europe and Japan have the problems of barnacled old institutions and entrenched university and political interests, at least as much as we do here. (After all, some major European universities date from the fourteenth century. Do the European systems carry proportionally more institutional baggage with their more advanced age?)

Other nations' solutions to these adaptive problems have been far from perfect. German science, despite its apparently enlightened institutional arrangements and stable funding, has generally been lackluster, with the exception of the highly productive all-German accelerator center, DESY, in Hamburg. Great Britain suffers from the basic-research-is-best syndrome, and its weakness in engineering and entrepreneurship discourages links between basic science and product innovation. Though trying to establish a high-quality basic science effort, Japan has run into resistance from its own universities. We can learn from these as we try our own adaptive experiment.

There is a third international factor which the political proclivities of the Reagan administration have made very clear. The free flow of information across national boundaries will be jeopardized, not only by companies seeking to lock up scientific ideas for their exclusive gain, but also by government security agencies in the name of conserving military advantage. Whether they are like the basic mathematicians at Stanford and the Massachusetts Institute of Technology who stumbled on the keys to unlocking many of the world's most advanced codes while working on basic prime number theory, or a small company in Vermont that grinds bearings which was accused of selling the Soviets the know-how secret to MIRV, U.S. scientists and engineers will collide with the government. They will have a duty to protect national security, but also a duty to resist untoward encroachments into the area of scientific communication. This will be another agenda item for the profession in this brave new world.

I

Good data on the international travels of U.S. scientists are difficult to obtain, so the trends we are discussing probably never can be proved conclusively. But statistics published by the National Research Council (NRC) and NATO do suggest an isolationist trend. Japan's rise to technological distinction in the last decade corresponds to the number of Japanese scientists who have traveled abroad. The NRC[2] indicates that Japan sent 2,526 scientists abroad in 1965, of which half went to North America. In 1980, Japan sent 8,870 abroad, of which 3,500 went to North America. Yet few foreign scientists visit Japan; in 1980 their total number was estimated at 732. Many more foreigners visited Japan briefly.[3]

In the 1970s, the percentage of U.S. doctorates planning to study abroad declined from 1.5 percent to 0.9 percent, according to another NRC report. *Science Indicators* says, "The decline in the number of U.S. postdoctoral students going abroad comes at a time when they could benefit from improved scientific facilities in Western Europe."[4]

Table 2 shows the number of U.S. participants in international scientific congresses declining by 47 percent of its 1972–1974 level, while participation by foreigners has declined by 14 percent.

Statistics also show the growing collaboration among Great Britain and the Western European nations; in the past 15 years, they have pooled resources more (although not always successfully) to come up to par with the United States. *Science Indicators 1980* indicates that the fraction of West German research papers

Table 2 U.S. and foreign participation in international scientific congresses*

2-Year period	Number of congresses	Number of participants		
		Total	U.S.	Non-U.S.
1960–62	23	33,082	9,033	24,049
1963–65	28	37,964	10,012	27,952
1966–68	42	59,748	12,297	47,451
1969–71	38	55,711	12,956	42,755
1972–74	73	73,819	18,630	55,189
1975–77	52	59,658	12,767	46,891
1978–80	37	55,358	7,975	47,383

* Source: National Science Foundation, Science Indicators Office.

co-authored with someone from another country increased from 36 percent to 44 percent in 1973–1979; in France the number of papers with non-French co-authors rose from 27 percent to 35 percent. In 1979, 40 percent of papers with British authors had non-British co-authors, up from 35 percent in 1973. Yet in the same period, the fraction of U.S. papers having foreign co-authors rose less, from 14 percent to 17 percent.[5]

This growth in European collaboration is a natural outgrowth of the expansion of European science organizations in the 1970s, including CERN, the Centre Européen pour la Recherche Nucléaire; EMBRO, the European Molecular Biology Research Organization at Heidelberg, founded in 1964; the European Space Agency, also founded in 1964; COST, for European scientific co-operation, founded by the European Economic Community in 1971; the European Science Foundation founded in 1974; and specific projects such as the Joint European Torus, JET, in Culham, Great Britain, a jointly sponsored fusion device. With Great Britain as the exception, European spending on science rose by 50 percent in real terms from 1965 to 1975.

Dorothy Shore Zinberg of the John F. Kennedy School of Government at Harvard is one of the few analysts of international scientific travel. She writes that the limited data that are available show that the most talented and productive scientists are much more likely to have traveled abroad than their less productive colleagues. She cited a study by Lipset and Ladd that found that 62 percent of the "high travelers" published twenty or more articles, whereas only 5 percent of the non-travelers did. Young U.S. postdocs who go abroad are likely to be of much higher quality than those who stay at home. Many well-known scientists, such as Nobel Prize winning physicist Steven Weinberg, have testified that their training abroad aided their intellectual development.

So why, these days, do so few go? Zinberg notes the changed values of recent students from the previous generation. Students now see their science and engineering degrees as a ticket to getting a job and are unmoved when their professors discourse on the intrinsic beauty of science. The preoccupation with getting a job inhibits them from going abroad during or after graduate school, when the competition for university jobs is toughest. Finally, the younger scientist or recent student is more apt to be married to someone starting a career of his or her own; for the couple to go to Europe for a year is a form of double jeopardy.[6]

Moreover, funding for such visits has declined. The number of coveted Fulbright scholarships, for which there were eighty-six applicants for a single opening in 1980–1981, has remained constant, while funding for the NATO Science Fellowships has eroded. Also, a structural change in federal science budgets cut down international travel. During the 1960s and early 1970s, U.S. scientists could pay for a 3- or 6-month, or a 1-year visit abroad from their regular federal research grants. But as funding has become tighter, there has been a tendency not to apply for overseas work. The National Science Foundation's Office of International Programs — the guardian of these arrangements — has been diminished. NSF's new policy is for the regular disciplinary programs to pick up the tab for foreign travel. But the tendency of NSF program managers, as always, is to fund as many projects at home as possible.

As U.S. scientists are getting less first-hand experience of foreign science, their leaders are engaging in frantic, sometimes high-handed, efforts to collaborate — and just as often to avoid collaborating — with foreign programs. This instability in our cooperative efforts can deter the Europeans and Japanese from joining with us and sometimes earns their scorn.

The United States dragged its heels on wholehearted cooperation with the European community in those areas where neither commercial nor security interests were involved, such as radioactive waste disposal. The Reagan administration has cut cooperative global climate studies, meanwhile trying to raise foreign contributions to the Deep Sea Drilling Program. One of the two satellites of the European–U.S. solar–polar mission was canceled by the United States, crippling the scientific usefulness of that key project to both U.S. and foreign participants, since many of the results depended on the synergism of having two. Postponements of key decisions on U.S. earth-imaging satellites has made some Europeans glad they have not counted on it, and thankful for their own earth-imaging satellite program. Harvey Brooks and Eugene Skolnikoff have noted, separately,[7] that the United States lacks an overall strategy for international scientific projects. Yet their importance will grow as telescopes, fusion devices, accelerators, and other large instruments become too costly for any one country — even the United States — to bear alone. Maybe the high cost of new machines will finally force internationalism on U.S. science.

II

Before discussing specific countries and their arrangement for science, a few propositions are in order. The United States should not wait to encourage its scientists to become interested in a country until that country's research is equal to or better than ours. This certainly was not a requirement earlier, in the 1960s, when the U.S. scientists traveled a lot. Thus, a program of outreach abroad should not be in the spirit of a "Help! We're behind!" (the attitude finally moving some U.S. companies to visit their counterparts in Japan). Scientific cooperation is a two-way street: the United States and foreign countries can help one another contribute to a common base of scientific knowledge. Fortunately, U.S. universities, with their doors flung open to foreign students, contribute handsomely to the exchange. A recent study at Harvard found that foreigners were among the best-performing students academically. More and more graduate students are foreign, as are more young faculty members, especially in engineering.

Some U.S. scientists have begun to look "over the parapet," as one of them said, across the ocean barriers that historically kept the United States apart, politically and economically, from other nations. Over that parapet may lie another frontier that U.S. science has barely begun to contemplate — a world of coequals in science.

Further, there are many science policy lessons to be learned. Does the United States want to go the way of Great Britain, with an elite engaged in high science while the country falters in developing a sound, technology-based economy? Should the United

States model itself on the present, highly integrated Japanese system of support for research in targeted areas and close negotiations with industry? What lessons are there in the regional approach followed in West Germany, where research policy is set by the *Länder* governments and relies on independent institutes serving both the universities and industry? A quick tour offers some tantalizing glimpses relevant to our management of science here at home.

Japan

Japan is now expanding its efforts in purposive basic and undirected basic research. Thus, it has recognized that work of a fundamental nature is a vital link in the cycle. As with everything else, the Japanese are studying how other countries do science. It will be interesting to see the result. Will Japanese science be better linked than U.S. science to national applied and industrial problems? Is the Japanese sequence of building up technology first and science after a tacit confirmation of Derek deSolla Price's view of science as proceeding from technology?

The casualness with which prominent U.S. scientists have dismissed Japanese science is amazing. In a few years, however, it may give way to near-panic that we must restructure our science to "catch up to" the Japanese. In fact, since the Meiji revolution of 1868, when Japanese universities were modeled along the lines of the old European ones, Japan has produced much good science. But until recently, it was all published in Japanese. Japanese science has been world-class when it has trained and equipped a critical mass of high-quality scientists. Nishina's cyclotron at Tokyo in the 1930s, for example, was frequently visited by the roving physicists of that day. Of the six Nobel Prizes awarded to Japanese, three have been in physics and one in chemistry.[8]

Justin Bloom, who was U.S. science attaché in Tokyo for 6 years, has written that the Japanese government now gives honors to young scientists to encourage individualism and creativity in the formative stages of their careers. The government is also trying to change the universities (which, being old, encrusted ivory towers, have not contributed much to Japan's postwar economic miracle) along the lines of Stanford or the Massachusetts Institute of Technology. There is an effort to change a rule barring foreigners from having tenure.

Yet some indication of the resistance encountered in trying to refashion basic science may be seen in the fact that the government had to start a new institution, Tsukuba Science City, outside Tokyo, to make a strong start in science. The science city may reflect the extent to which entrenched interests have been an obstacle to reform. The city masses nearly half of Japan's research effort in one place, meant to produce "critical mass" science of high quality. The concept of the "science city" first used by the Soviets in Novosibirsk, with its emphasis on critical mass, multidisciplinarity, and localized technology transfer, is being considered in other countries and may have relevance for the United States, as we describe in the last chapter.[9]

Japan's science city, high-energy physics, and medical research, its new 25-meter radio telescope, and its infusion of funds into biotechnology signal a serious push in science. In addition, more Japanese scientists are publishing in English-language journals, which will make their work known in the West. The dates when Japanese scientists won their Nobels in science, 1949, 1965, 1973, and 1981, suggest that Japan's investment in basic science may be already starting to pay off. How will U.S. scientists feel if Japan starts turning out top quality science, along with better television sets and automobiles?

As for the links to applications, Japan's interventionist government technology policy helps. As Jack Baranson and Harald Malmgren have written,[10] in the United States,

> technology policy has two broad components; first, maintenance of and a technological lead in areas of vital concern to national security; and second, maintenance of an economic environment that enables the private sector to pursue its own technological avenues of exploration on a competitive basis. There are also selected areas, aside from defense and space, such as in medical research and certain university research programs where the policy has been to give public support to research, but this has been of lesser importance. . . .

In some other nations, technology policy is aimed at strengthening basic research and at strengthening the competitiveness of key industries. But in other nations the perception of technology policy is much broader, and constitutes part of a more general "vision" of how the economy should be structured in the future.

The best known example of Japan's approach is MITI, the Ministry of International Trade and Industry (note the contrast with our own, passively titled, Department of Commerce). MITI's plan, titled "Vision" for the 1980s,

is not an economic plan, however. It is rather a consensus view of what is likely, and what should be emphasized if the Japanese economy is to continue its rapid structural adjustment to changing global realities.

Most accounts stress the slowness of change in Japan and the gradual evolution of consensus. But most of Japan's success stories have come from vigorous government restructuring of key policies, institutions, and industries — a striking contrast with the U.S. government's attitude of intervening primarily to bail out companies that are in trouble. Since 1868 when the Meiji restoration undertook to force Japan to catch up to the rest of the world, the government has assumed responsibility for managing industrial change. As its industry matured and became self-sufficient, the government stood back and allowed more free play among rival Japanese companies. It offers nudging patronage, catalytic research, and occasional knocking together of heads.[11]

Figure 13 shows how the Japanese government supports science and technology. The tradition of government responsibility for industrial policy and the vertical integration of the government make it eager to subsidize industrial R&D or undertake research too risky for one company or a group of companies. Japanese R&D tends to be based on 7- to 10-year plans, and companies often undertake research in parallel with each other and with government.

A range of mechnisms, from the *shingikai* (advisory councils) to the *genkyoku* (the government bureau that guides, regardless of its specific authority), and the plans, or "visions," assure

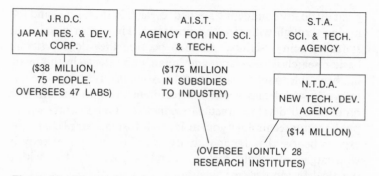

Figure 13 "Japan Inc." is no monolith when it comes to research. Several Japanese science agencies directly fund industry research, and their own in-house work on generic technology and applied science. Ministry of Education support of university science not shown. (BASED ON: Jack Baranson and Harald B. Malmgren, "Technology and Trade Policy: Issues and an Agenda for Action," Washington, D.C., 1981, prepared for the U.S. Department of Labor and the Office of the U.S. Trade Representative.)

thoroughness and consistency in working toward long-term goals. Moreover, the companies are eager to have the government crutch withdrawn once a technology matures into a product. Many successful Japanese products have appeared when a company found a better version than the officially sponsored one and marketed it on its own.

The entire system is *not* intended to put industrial development on one side and government-supported basic research on the other, as the United States does. It is a tense but symbiotic relationship between the government, trade associations (which undertake joint research), and industry. Japan's system is no monolith: seen from the inside it is characterized by intense rivalries and furious politicking over major decisions.

Japanese public sector technology programs are instructive for the United States: as we said earlier, the United States has fallen down. Japan has effective research and development on harbor and river management, postal service, high-speed rail, fire prevention, and earthquake engineering. The United States has had great difficulty conducting applied research in these areas and following through with effective programs. They never acquire the status of being "serious" research because they do not fit our basic-research-is-best paradigm. Japan, unburdened by this myth, has been able to set consistent goals, assign institutions to the job, integrate social and economic requirements into the research process, and develop practical technology. One recently agreed public sector technology goal in Japan is fusion: some U.S. fusion experts believe that Japan's ability to follow through effectively with large-scale public sector research will make it first with a practical fusion device.

Overall, the contrast between research policy in Japan and in the United States is striking. In Japan, the government has an old and proven role in research in key industrial fields. This has enabled MITI to rescue old industries such as steel and shipbuilding by transforming them. Even when a major industry, such as computers, begins doing well, MITI has been dissatisfied that it was not pushing hard enough. Yet the U.S. government makes a point of *not* doing applied research in fields where U.S. industry is strong. George A. Keyworth II, the President's science adviser, is adamant about cutting such programs.

Federal Republic of Germany

Both postwar West German industry and science have enjoyed extraordinary revivals. Through the mid-1970s, both enjoyed stability and prosperity, as in the 1960s in the United States. Postwar German scientists have won several Nobel Prizes, although German science is a long way from its prewar eminence. More recently, however, as major industries, such as chemicals, have been having a harder time, and as economic conditions have worsened and unemployment has risen, the German government has asked whether it is getting enough innovation and productivity for its investment in science and technology.

The German research system[12] bears some resemblance to that of the United States in its wealth and diversity. Fundamental and applied research is sponsored by government and industry in approximately fifty prestigious nonprofit Max Planck Institutes and in their applied counterparts, the Fraunhofer institutes, which are concerned with transferring new knowledge to industrial applications, and approximately sixty industrial research institutes run under the auspices of the AIF, the Federation of Industrial Research Associations.

But German research is mainly governed by regional authorities, not Bonn, and by key individuals in local research institutes. Consistent with the postwar constitution, very little authority for science and technology is in the hands of the federal government; the governments of the Länder, or states, contribute one-fourth to one-half of the funds for the main science funding agency, DFG, or Deutsche Forschungsgemeinschaft. Together, they pay the salaries of university researchers and sponsor much work at the institutes. Most universities are well enough supported to be able to undertake modest research efforts from their own pockets, so to speak: government funding is sought for larger or collaborative projects or those falling in areas selected for Schwerpunkt, or priority attention.[13] Overall priorities and even specific decisions are decided by the Wissenschaftsrat, a science council that includes representatives of the universities, the institutes, the federal and Länder governments, and industry. The Wissenschaftsrat's decisions are technically not binding, but because they represent a broad and authoritative consensus, they are in effect.

Those concerned about the instability of individual U.S. project grants may find the German system interesting. The majority of DFG funds is awarded for long-term projects: one-third of this budget, or $350 million per year, goes to 1- to 3-year project grants. From an estimated 5,000 proposals received, panels of elected peer reviewers pick which shall be funded: the decisions of the peers are all supposed to be made in a single, 3-month period, although it has stretched longer on occasion. The DFG's "special collaborative research programs" are awarded to university groups for 10-year periods, with 3-year evaluations. Smaller groups of researchers requiring special support can qualify as Forschergruppes and receive funding for 5-year periods.

Bruce L. R. Smith and Charles V. Kidd, who examined the German research system on behalf of the U.S. National Research

Council, concluded that this overall stability causes many German observers to believe that the U.S. system generates a measure of "wasted motion." The German system includes a certain number of individual, short-term project grants, but in general they are much less important than the long-term awards mentioned above.

Smith and Kidd pointed out that the stability of the German system has both strengths and weaknesses. On the one hand, the fact that most senior researchers have good jobs and high salaries means they tend not to move about: this creates fewer openings for younger scientists. Some Germans believe that the frenetic short-term pace of funding in the United States gives us an edge in being able to respond to fast-moving developments. On the other hand, as we saw, it also makes us drop unglamorous areas which may be of long-term importance.[14]

Great Britain

Undirected basic research in Great Britain has been excellent despite tight budgets that have hacked away at it for years. No other country has so many Nobel Prizes per inhabitant. How British science remains excellent on so little money may be relevant to U.S. science, which may never again, in absolute terms, see the phenomenal growth in funding it had in the good old days of the 1960s. Part of the answer is Britain's high concentrations of talent in a few institutions.

British science in universities[15] generally follows the basic-research-is-best model described in Chapters 1 and 2. Despite the growth of the red brick universities in the 1960s and of established technical schools such as Imperial College, Great Britain has not had a strong system of basic-cum-applied institutions comparable to the U.S. land-grant colleges, Stanford, or M.I.T. A major problem has been engineering, which has been outstanding only in some circumscribed pockets of British industry. National attitudes die hard: part of the "British disease," as it is called there, is that country's disdain for engineering. Several remedial steps to recognize the importance of engineering have not overcome this problem.

Thus, while the British have invented many things — from the jet engine to the basic technique for producing monoclonal antibodies — the infrastructure for the *interconnections* between applied science, small innovative firms, and domestic markets has not been available to bring them to market. The environment for British research, then, differs substantially from that in the United States. In addition, innovation and development in several key industries — nuclear power, coal, and steel among them — have been affected by the fact that they are government-owned.

Government policies have tried to establish links between science and applications, but with mixed success. Several changes sprang from the 1972 Rothschild report which urged closer relations between the science agencies and the mission or "customer" agencies of government. The National Research Development Corporation was successful in the 1970s in licensing new technology, but it was also accused of not doing enough for small firms; it has now been merged into the new British Technology Group. Another mechanism is the Advisory Council for Applied Research and Development, a committee of eminent scientists supposed to alert the Secretary of State for Education and Science about emerging fields such as biotechnology. The British government has also in the past stepped in and set up high-tech industries in the hope they would bear fruit, such as the ICL in computers and Celltech in biotechnology.

How has British science maintained excellence despite awesome austerity? Smith and Kidd concluded that selectivity has been key. The University Grants Committee (UGC) and five national research councils have been careful to protect the critical mass centers, such as Oxford and Cambridge, even when this has drastic implications for other, less fortunate, institutions. They wrote:

Competition for research funds and for recognition among geographic regions and among different types of universities is less intense in Britain than in the United States, and cultural attitudes allow for deference to recognized elite groups more readily in Britain than in the United States.[16]

Great Britain's example raises the question, however, of

whether the United States should continue to staff more than ten or twelve first-ranked basic research institutions, which is what it has tried to do for the past 20 years. Great Britain may simply be more realistic with respect to human resources. We, resisting elitism more, may distribute resources more democratically, but end by spreading them too thin.

In addition, the UGC and the research councils have responded to austerity with measures to promote stability. Overall spending levels are determined at 3-year intervals. Once the UGC has told the schools how much money each will receive, it is largely up to them to decide how to spend it (with some exceptions, however). Thus, an average faculty member at a top British university is in an enviable position, in some ways, compared to his or her U.S. counterpart. British faculty members earn far less and, except at Oxbridge, they have nothing like their U.S. colleagues in the way of instrumentation and often have to share with other laboratories and schools. Nonetheless, the government's, the university's, and their own research priorities are known for 3 years, so their time and energy are not consumed scrambling for the next grant. An interesting feature of the British system is the extent to which it has come to rely on international, cooperative projects to permit scientists to work on large-scale instruments. The Science and Engineering Research Council, which funds fundamental scientific work, spends 28 percent of its budget on international cooperative programs such as CERN. Approximately 16 percent of the combined budgets of all the councils are devoted to such projects. (If the U.S. National Science Foundation were to spend 28 percent of its budget on international projects, the sum would be $360 million per year!)

III

But at a time when U.S. scientists should be traveling abroad more, U.S. security agencies are becoming more concerned about the "leaks" of sensitive U.S. technical information abroad. Both the Carter and Reagan administrations have been involved in efforts to curb academic research in the name of national security.

The incidents started under President Carter. The most notorious one was a clumsy attempt by an employee of the National Security Agency (NSA) to stop a group of mathematicians from discussing prime numbers theory at a meeting of the Institute of Electrical and Electronics Engineers (IEEE) information group. The employee, J. A. Meyer, wrote to the IEEE suggesting that open presentation of certain mathematical concepts at the meeting might violate the International Traffic in Arms Regulations (ITAR), a body of rules dating from the 1950s and applying mostly to military hardware exports. As can happen in science, these particular mathematicians had stumbled on an interesting set of problems which facilitated the construction of very hard-to-break codes. Since NSA's job is to crack foreign codes around the world and to assure the security of U.S. codes, it was alarmed that the spread of this fundamental knowledge would enable unsophisticated countries with a few good mathematicians to make their codes extremely hard to break.

Under ITAR, the scientific findings in spoken or published form might constitute "technical data" — a term usually applied to instructions accompanying a shipment of military hardware. Although it was unclear that the scientists' work was indeed covered by ITAR, the threat of government action was sufficiently serious to prompt elaborate negotiations between representatives of the NSA and the university community. In the end, a set of voluntary policies was agreed upon by all sides.[17] (Knowledge of this kind indeed seems to be coming to have direct economic value. The mathematical work would be an excellent tool for a business wishing to keep its secrets. Likely commercial applications, it was said at the time, would come in banking and petroleum.)

ITAR's long arm extended itself again during the Carter years when the Defense Advanced Research Projects Agency (DARPA) launched a $200 million, 5-year program in very high speed integrated circuits (VHSIC), which are critical in many military systems and in electronics generally. A number of major universities were eager to win shares of the VHSIC program, to do unclassified work that would also be at the breaking edge of a vital, fast-moving field. However, the House Armed Services Committee inserted into the bill authorizing the program the stipulation that it was to be carried out within the ITAR framework. Technically, this meant that those receiving government funds under the program would have to police their participants to be sure no "technical data" — which could mean scientific information generally — flowed overseas without prior State Department permission. This was an absurd precondition for the conduct of university science, since university researchers publish their work openly and talk about it in their laboratories, corridors, and cafeterias — and at meetings.

Reagan administration defense officials went further, interpreting the authorization language to mean that no foreign nationals should work on DOD-sponsored VHSIC research on campus — which could have made the work very difficult indeed, as perhaps as many as half of all assistants in computer science on campus these days are foreigners. This move drew a sharp protest from the presidents of five major research universities, and subsequent negotiations.[18]

There were other incidents. Organizers of an international conference on bubble memories sponsored by the American Vacuum Society in February 1980 were told that under ITAR and the related Export Administration Regulations (EAR) they would have to disinvite participants from the Soviet Union, Eastern Europe, and China because they should have obtained prior permission from the Commerce Department and had not done so. In the end, only the Chinese managed to attend (partly because the State Department did not want to strain relations at that moment) and only on the condition that the meeting discuss only data in the public literature or general trends in research. Other foreign scientists attending were to sign a guarantee that they would not pass on the information they learned at the meeting to Eastern Bloc nations.

The Reagan administration eagerly extended such measures. A Soviet computer scientist was told he could visit Stanford University only if he would limit himself to the mechanical theory of robot locomotion, and did not see control units, programming techniques, or industrial work in the field. The administration issued a new executive order that gave the government the authority to classify at birth — i.e., no matter where in the United States it originated — basic research findings it considered of national security importance. This was a legal authority which, for 25 years, had existed only in the field of atomic energy and even there was of questionable constitutionality. At the last minute before a major meeting of the Society of Photo-Optical Instrumentation Engineers, a large number of the prospective speakers were informed by the DOD that they should have submitted their papers to DOD for prior clearance and, lacking DOD permission, should not give them. Officials discussed establishing gray areas of unclassified university research which might be considered sensitive anyway, that DOD might censor.[19]

All of this raised, quite properly, loud protests from university officials and a major attempt to define whether there was indeed a problem of "leakage" of a militarily sensitive nature from university research. This took the form of a major study by the National Academy of Sciences released in 1982. This study, known as the Corson Report, found that the problem of leakage of U.S. technical information in sensitive areas stemmed overwhelmingly from sources other than U.S. university campuses. Nonetheless, the report foresaw a long and difficult period of strain and conflict between university scientists and the national security establishment.[20]

Clearly, the scientific profession faces another challenge to its long-standing goals and values. Maintaining high standards of academic freedom may be very difficult in the years ahead.

NOTES

[1] *Science Indicators 1982* (National Science Board, 1983), pp. 29–31 and Fig. 1-23.

[2] *International Mobility of Scientists and Engineers*, Report of a workshop sponsored by NATO Science Committee, European Science Foundation, held in Lisbon, Portugal, 22–25 June 1981, published by the U.S. National Research Council, p. 75. Hereafter referred to as NRC, *International Mobility*.

[3] NRC, *International Mobility*, p. 145.

⁴ Summary Report 1979 Doctorate Recipients from United States Universities (Washington, D.C.: Commission on Human Resources, National Research Council, 1980), pp. 4–12. See *Science Indicators*, National Science Board, 1981, p. 41.

⁵ *Science Indicators 1980*, Report of the National Science Board, 1981, pp. 41–47.

⁶ Dorothy Shore Zinberg, "America and Europe – Changing Patterns of Science-Related Travel," *Issues and Current Studies*, National Research Council, 1980, pp. 111–121.

⁷ Harvey Brooks, "The Changing Structure of the U.S. Research System," a talk given to George Washington University science policy seminar, November 1982. Author's file. Eugene B. Skolnikoff, "The Insularity of Our Science and Technology Policy," a talk given in November 1982, George Washington University science policy. Author's files.

⁸ Justin Bloom, "Japanese Science and Technology," in *Speaking of Japan*, 2:5 (August 1981), pp. 29, 30.

⁹ Justin Bloom, *op. cit.*, p. 27. Justin L. Bloom and Shinsuke Asano, "Tsukuba Science City: Japan Tries Planned Innovation," *Science*, 212 (12 June 1981), pp. 1239ff.

¹⁰ Jack Baranson and Harold B. Malmgren, *Technology and Trade Policy: Issues and an Agenda for Action* (Washington, D.C., 1981), pp. 6, 7.

¹¹ Baranson and Malmgren, *op. cit.*, pp. 62–64. See also Patricia Hagan Kunwayama, "Success Story," *The Wilson Quarterly*, Winter 1982, pp. 133–144.

¹² "Research in Europe and the United States," Chap. 13 of *Outlook* Research Council, W. H. Freeman & Co., 1982, pp. 545–559. Researched by Bruce L. R. Smith and Charles V. Kidd. Hereafter referred to as *Outlook*, Chapter 13.

¹³ Baranson and Malmgren, op. cit., pp. 42–43. Also, *Outlook*, Chapter 13, pp. 550–554. A good description of German science and its problems is *Nature* (27 May 1982), p. 261ff.

¹⁴ *Outlook*, Chapter 13, pp. 557–559, 569.

¹⁵ *Outlook*, Chapter 13, pp. 520–533. Also Baranson and Malmgren,

¹⁶ *Outlook*, Chapter 13, p. 522.

¹⁷ A good narrative of the growing intrusions into university science

by U.S. national security authorities is in David Dickson, *The New Politics of Science* (New York: Pantheon Books, 1984), pp. 141–145.

[18] *Ibid.,* pp. 145–149.

[19] *Ibid.,* pp. 149–151.

[20] "Scientific Communication and National Security," Panel on Scientific Communication and National Security, Committee on Science, Engineering and Public Policy (Washington, D.C.: National Academy Press, 1982), Volumes 1 and 2.

6
Science and Society: The New Contract

I T IS APPROPRIATE to close this essay, whose starting point was the threshold on which Bush and his colleagues stood in 1945, with a look at the threshold we stand on today. In 1985, after the sobering 1960s and 1970s, many Americans are starting to feel a cooler version of the excitement of the immediate postwar period, that a new age is dawning, characterized by the unparalleled impact of science and technology on our economic system and its products, and on our leisure, work, health, and old age. Even a few science policy professors have been asking whether teaching the proper rationale for federal funding of basic research – the core of traditional science policy – ignores key changes in our society and no longer qualifies a student as a modern oracle of Delphi.

For a moment let us put ourselves in the position Bush and the others stood in 40 years ago and look to the future in order to design new arrangements for science appropriate to today's needs. We see a need for a greatly simplified basic science system, aimed at the twin goals of doing world-class science and linkage to society, and, at the same time, the reconfiguration of most university research towards excellence in long-term applied science.

First, we look into the future. It doesn't matter whose view of the future we pick, since much conventional wisdom about it these days is running along similar lines (except for those who forecast — perhaps rightly — that we will all be destroyed by either nuclear war or high federal deficits). Arbitrarily, let us look at the vision of the future put forward in John Naisbitt's best-selling book, *Megatrends*. We pick it not because we have conducted a multi-million dollar, 3-year research project to imagine the future and have become to the same conclusions as Naisbitt, but because the book obviously rings true to many Americans — 4 million to be exact, who have snapped it up since it was first published in 1982.

I

Megatrends or any of a number of other futures documents is a useful vehicle for re-asking the questions Bush faced in 1945. What needs will society have for basic research, purposive basic research, applied science, engineering, and development for the next 15 years? How, therefore, should science be structured to serve those needs? What personnel will we need in terms of Ph.D.s, M.S.s, and B.S.s? What will we need in the way of technicians, accountants, lawyers, and even doctors, some of whose specialties will be rendered obsolete by technology? And, to return to the main theme of this essay, what will be needed in the way of institutional arrangements? What should be the structure and values for the profession of science?

To answer these questions rigorously *would* require a multi-million dollar, 3-year research grant. But we have already reserved the right in this essay to be outrageously unscientific and play our hunches, aided by our experience, research, and exchange of ideas with experts. And, as we said in Chapter 1, a theater critic does not have to write the next night's script. Critics can also write about the future of the theater without having to actually discover the next Shakespeare.

But back to *Megatrends*. The main point it shares with other thinking about the future is that our formerly industrial society is not only turning into Daniel Bell's "post-industrial" society but into an "information" society as well. Naisbitt writes that 60 percent of the U.S. work force has jobs involving the creation, processing or distribution of information. He includes in this category programmers, teachers, clerks, secretaries, accountants, stock brokers, managers, insurance people, bureaucrats, lawyers, bankers, and technicians.[1] In 1950 only 17 percent of the U.S. work force held jobs that he considers information jobs. Contrary to popular wisdom, our service sector is *not* growing; it has remained at approximately one-tenth the total work force for some time. The big drop, he claims, is in manufacturing, which employs only 13 percent of the work force. "We are working ourselves out of the manufacturing business and into the thinking business," says David Birch, who compiled these figures, in the book.

Naisbitt tosses out several ideas which are not overly original but which, taken together, should give scientists food for thought. For example:

- *The microprocessor revolution* (we saw its beginnings in Bell Laboratories in Chapter 3) *is creating more and more databases that will swamp editors and journals and change traditional publishing, especially publications whose rationale is the transfer of information.* (We saw signs of this in the growth of scientific journals in Chapter 4.

- *As we drown in data we starve for knowledge.* (This echoes our view of the greater need for synthesis across subspecialties and disciplines, and the problems of disaggregating science into hundreds of thousands of isolated "cells" of information.)

- *The information "float" is collapsing*; i.e., the time it takes for information to be generated to the time the world learns of it is becoming instantaneous thanks to communications. (This should interest science policy analysts who assume that it *must* take 30 years from the time of a basic research discovery to the introduction of a new product based on it. Thirty years by what immutable law? Will this collapse of the information "float" change the traditional, loose relationship between science and innovation?)

- *As society becomes more high-tech, and more in need of people with advanced skills and knowledge, the educational*

system has turned out an increasingly inferior product.
(There is already a yawning gap between the Ph.D. microbiologist who moves forward with his advancing field and the high school biology student who may become a technician using the Ph.D.'s invention. Things will get worse, not better, because the Ph.D.'s field advances faster than the high school biology curriculum can.)

- *We will have less demand for the specialist who is soon obsolete and more need for the generalist who can adapt.* (Medical education has become an orgy of specialized courses, taught by professors seeking to cram as many data as possible from their own specialty into the brains of students who are already overworked. A recent study by the American Association of Medical Colleges asked: shouldn't we be teaching future M.D.s how to teach themselves?)

Naisbitt's thoughts are hardly the stuff of systematic analysis — and our parenthetical comments aren't either. But they offer new perspectives on the future of science, technology, and education. If you believe for the moment that journals will be virtually obsolete, that syntheses across specialties will be far more important than specialization, that scientific knowledge will turn more rapidly into innovation, and that the mass of people will get more, rather than less, technologically illiterate, then the future of science looks to be a brand-new sleigh ride!

There are, to be sure, problems with Naisbitt's text. He sometimes uses the words "knowledge" and "information" interchangeably, though they represent rather different things. Sometimes he uses the term "know-how," when either knowledge or information would be better. Know-how means what Derek deSolla Price called "brains in their fingertips" and is not the synthesis of data that is knowledge. Like other authors who write about the future, he has disturbingly little to say about science and gives no hint of having any knowledge of it. Maybe the science profession should be asking: Why are the Peters and Watermans and the Naisbitts — who tout the revolution technology will bring — so ignorant of science? Is it another sign of the divorce between science and technology that has got us in so much hot water already?

Nonetheless, Naisbitt does make a central point which is of importance to the structure and values of the science profession. It is that knowledge is coming to represent economic value, directly.

> In an industrial society, the strategic resource is capital. . . . But in our new society, as Daniel Bell first pointed out, the strategic resource is information. Not the only resource, but the most important. . . .
>
> The new source of power is not money in the hands of a few but information in the hands of the many. . . .
>
> Unlike other forces in the universe . . . knowledge is not subject to the law of conservation: It can be created, it can be destroyed, and most importantly it is synergetic—that is, the whole is usually greater than the sum of its parts. . . . *In an information economy, then, value is increased not by labor, but by knowledge.* [Italics added][2]

Is it possible that the value of products is coming to depend on the scientific knowledge they embody? Many of the hottest new products have knowledge embedded in them, specific knowledge, that is, which is different from the specific knowledge embedded in a rival product. The customer buys the product for the specific knowledge that makes it different from its rival. In other words, the specific knowledge in the product, which is often scientific in nature, is what gives the product economic value.

When a hospital department orders one type of monoclonal antibodies, or MABS (these are proteins which can be genetically engineered to detect a particular disease in the body), from one biotechnology firm, it selects on the basis of the particular structure of the MABS that makes them better than the competing, differently grown MABS offered by a rival firm.

When a family picks a home computer, it selects largely on the basis of the software the computer can use—software probably invented by some pale-faced, 20-year-old representative of the Atari generation in his or her basement. And the knowledge "trick" embedded in that software is bought by the family because it is seen better than the "trick" offered by a rival software company and invented by someone who was, perhaps, 21 years old.

The argument works better for computers and biotechnology than for other industries. Nonetheless, the idea of a steady differentiation of products by their scientific content may be a useful way to consider the relationship between science and industry in the future.

Let us end this discussion of *Megatrends* with one further thought. Knowledge increases economic value, Naisbitt says, mainly in dozens of small high-tech enterprises jockeying with one another in the thousands of markets created by society's transition to an information society. So the scientists will have to contend with volatility, competition, fast-paced product development, quick shifts in market strategy, and sudden returns to the drawing board, which is the laboratory. These are the characteristics of the thousands of electronics and biotechnology firms at the forefront of this technological revolution. Nonetheless, if these fast-paced, diversified, science-intensive industries become the norm, business will become more dependent on science than ever. In short, university scientists may be dragged from their ivory towers by the entrepreneurs, whether they like it or not.

II

If this is to be the future, what arrangements should there be for the conduct of basic research? How can the linkages between science and applications be assured and strengthened? How should university scientists conceive of their profession, since they probably thought back in graduate school that they were choosing a path remote from the messy world of meeting payrolls, profit and loss statements, and leveraged buy-outs? How should the government structure itself and its support of science? What role should the states play? We will answer these questions with a few, broad-brush proposals that extend the approach put forward in this essay. But first, we summarize the problems:

- *Federal science institutions and policy have great difficulty fostering strong links between basic and applied science.* The good side of the postwar science structure included the care given to erect healthy, strong basic science, and the pluralism of funding agencies. Nonetheless, the pride of place given to basic research has cost us dear in applied science, in demonstration projects, and in getting industry to use government research.

The federal government has been outstandingly successful with some missions — mostly in defense and space, where a strong organizational effort was made and where success in application was the primary goal. But research difficulties, as much as policy constraints, have hindered the federal government from achieving new energy technologies, good high-speed transit, safer, stronger buildings and highways, and other public sector needs.

Moreover, the federal sector is now encrusted with institutions and political constituencies which, like old barnacles, prevent the ship from sailing smoothly through the water to some needed, applied goal. The Reagan philosophy toward civilian demonstration programs of "let industry do it" is a prescription for policy neglect, sudden cutbacks, and further instability in programs that desperately need the same kind of talent, organization, and attention now given to defense and some space programs.

- *Industry suffers from the neglect of purposive basic and applied science too.* The separation of basic science and applications that the profession has fostered has spread into industry, and robbed many U.S. companies of the expertise they need about the technologies on which they are based. Executives remain lacking in both knowledge and know-how, and even recent increases in industry research funds may represent bookkeeping to save taxes (thus increasing immediate profits) as much as a serious commitment to research. Staying power in industrial research is critical, a sine qua non: it is better to water and fertilize thirty apple trees in an orchard for ten years than to plant a hundred one year and cut them down the next.
- *Much university research talent is poorly used.* Encouraged

by 30 years of professional mythology to play the basic science game, many mid-ranked departments and institutions have a diffuse basic science effort and little heart in the applied science they do. The myth prevails of divorce between the two, of incompatibility, that "applied science inevitably drives out the pure." The result is dissipation of energy, low morale, and a morbid fixation on funding trends in Washington. Those companies reaching out to universities may find, to their disappointment, that the culture of basic-science-is-best is so deeply rooted that the professors see the relationship as research support, not a true partnership.

- *The science profession is partly responsible for the poor state of science education.* Yet it has a clear, long-term interest in the scientific literacy of the public that pays the bill — just as doctors have a stake in public education about disease, diet, and occupational hazards.
- *Our basic science system has deep, structural problems that prevent it from being as creative as it should be.* We are used to dwelling on its successes. But think how much more successful it could be if it had critical mass, highest-quality centers, with adequate funding, the best new instrumentation, and a freedom from the dead hand of bureaucracy that stands between creative scientists and their work. Money is not the answer, for even rising federal budgets will not compensate for the fast-rising cost of instrumentation, for the need to pay good salaries, for the need to have stability and a sense of fun to attract the best people and keep them creative. Moreover, decades of preaching by the profession about science for science's sake have left those practitioners who cannot compete in high science with low morale.
- *Finally, fundamental knowledge is an international good instantly transmitted around the world, and available to the first user to snap it up. But many applications of that knowledge become industrial property or have national security significance.* The tension between the need for communication among scientists of different nations, while their governments compete with one another over technology, will

not go away. It will get worse, and the profession must cope, and fight for the free flow of knowledge against increasingly difficult odds.

These, then, are the problems which should be overcome in designing a better structure for science.

III

Many reforms could be undertaken on the basis of the analysis offered earlier. The problems we have identified — particularly the snobbism of university science toward applications, toward engineering, toward industrial research — are deeply ingrained. Enormous effort will be required for attitudes to change. Perhaps only the shock of another nation, such as Japan, moving ahead in science *and* applications will bring about change. To be effective, change will have to come at the level of the working scientist: U.S. science can be only as fruitful as its individual practitioners. The people who speak for science at the top cannot legislate change by fiat or mere talk. On the other hand, they have enormous influence in persuading federal officials and members of Congress where to devote their time and policy attention.

Because this essay is an experiment, an attempt to review the play the morning after, we close with sample recommendations. The following list is broad brush and not exhaustive; it aims to show how many fruitful new approaches there are to draw from once it is conceded that the goals of the overall system must change. We hope our list shows, however imperfectly, that basic and applied science can work together better for the good of the nation, while pressing its quest at the endless frontier.

Since the proposals are so general, we should say what we seek to accomplish, namely: (1) to introduce a semblance of order and integrity to federal civilian applied programs in order to manage better the links between science and public sector technologies; (2) to strengthen industrial research so it can better anchor its activities in science to have the technical edge it needs; (3) to make the university science system as productive as possible,

Breaking out of the old paradigm. (SOURCE: Nalimov, p. 11.)

both of the best-trained students and of whatever kind of science, basic or applied, is done; (4) to give scientists themselves some sense of direction and morale, so that they will be no longer adrift; and (5) to rescue international scientific communication from the barriers imposed by national security and economic competition and improve the technical understanding of laymen.

To do all this requires changing the science system's values away from basic-research-is-best to science-for-society.

We have six proposal areas, each aimed at remedying the willful divorce between basic science and applications and the resulting problems of applied science.

1. At the federal level, greater integration is essential in the planning and execution of large civilian applied science and development programs. To achieve this we propose **an independent advisory board** attached to the Office of Management and Budget (OMB). The board would be made up of research managers from industry, universities, and government. Their terms would exceed the President's 4-year term to give them political independence. Yet because of their relationship to OMB, they would have authority to articulate *national* science and technology policy.

Vannevar Bush wrote in 1945, "We have no national policy for science," and his words are true today. We glimpsed the problem in the ceramic engine story in Chapter 3, and in some of the problems agricultural research has had lately. In short, there is now little counterweight to the forces of competition, disorganization, and pork barrel that can rob these programs—which are often large and of great national importance—of any semblance of effectiveness.

In a well-known pair of *Minerva* articles in 1963 and 1964, Alvin M. Weinberg criticized the "free interplay" by which the science community prefers to allocate resources:

> Because we have always arrived at an allocation by the free play of countervailing pressures this does not mean that such free interplay is the best or the only way to make choices.

Weinberg rejected a "supreme tribunal" making such choices as a myth (and we agree). Nonetheless, he insisted, some method for making scientific choices must be found, if only because:

> If those actively engaged in science do not make choices, then they will be made anyhow by the Congressional Appropriations Committees and by the Bureau of the Budget, or corresponding bodies in other governments.[3]

While Weinberg was speaking mainly of choices within science, rather than choices among federal research programs, we find these admonitions appropriate. Our board would hardly be a "supreme tribunal" but it would seek to guide, in the name of the national interest.

One of our chief concerns in this essay has been with the neglect of applied science, i.e., our inability to produce effective usable technology within the federal system so much of the time. This stems in part, we believe, from the traditional science policy's neglect of the *linkages* between science and applications. Yet in every story of the successful translation of science into technology we have seen (the Manhattan Project, penicillin, the Polaris-Poseidon program, Bell Labs), there has been an organizing intelligence, institutionally expressed.

The need for some sort of guidance has long been recognized. Philip M. Smith of the National Academy of Sciences wrote a useful study of various postwar science boards,[4] which, in effect, describes their consistent failure to exert leverage over the government's sprawling civilian science programs. The Federal Council for Science and Technology, for instance, was meant to coordinate in the active sense but has been reduced to brokering among bureaucrats. The National Science Board (NSB) had a mandate to review and pass on other departments' research programs, which was never fulfilled, as we saw. Smith writes that each science program has its own organizational base. So the pressures to bring all disputes to the top are enormous, usually to the Office of Science and Technology Policy (OSTP) in the White House. All this "underlying complexity," as Smith euphemistically calls it, is the subject of frequent calls for central guidance which have never been carried out.

In our view, the OSTP and Presidential Science Adviser, like the President's Science Advisory Committee (PSAC), have a primary job of winning the President's confidence and keeping it, which is distinct from the *national*, independent expert guidance we seek. PSAC has always taken the "P" and the "A" in its title too seriously to play this role—though it has, on occasion, shaped some federal programs decisively.

Our board would not engage in national planning, or make industrial policy. But it would draw on the experience of the Ministry of Trade and Industry (MITI) in Japan, which doesn't do these things either, as we saw in Chapter 5. Like MITI, it would not run research itself, but would articulate "visions" to which government and private industry could respond and outline policies for implementing these visions. In short, it would do the job of guiding national science policy Bush assigned to the "nine wise heads" in *Science—The Endless Frontier.*

Briefly, it would have five functions: (a) It would provide independent judgments on how to orchestrate technical programs. Disagreements with Presidential policy would be closely watched by the outside, much as the Council of Economic Advisers is meant to look after the overall economic health of the nation, as distinct from the President's immediate policies. (b) It would monitor the progress of regional technology efforts, described below, and perhaps advise on ways the federal government could help such efforts, where appropriate. (c) The board would play a vital role in building industry–government consensus on each sector's role in a particular technology or reaching a particular goal. For this, it could draw on the experience of the National Advisory Committee for Aeronautics, described earlier. (d) It would monitor the status of science education in the nation and advise on federal and local efforts. (e) Finally, it would try to bring order, and a long-term view, to government plans for international scientific cooperation, which are currently a source of much difficulty in our present political system.

2.   Second, we need to strengthen, or create where they have not existed, **sound, science-based companies** that are vital and technologically nimble enough to compete internationally in the decades ahead. Fortunately, in the thousands of small U.S. high-tech companies, in Bell Laboratories, and in other places, U.S. industry has suitable models. The problem will be to change the nature of management's expertise and concerns, and to reorganize inside, and to some extent between, companies to build a strongly linked fabric of science and technology.

Industrial managers should reorient their priorities (as some are already doing) to understand what their products are, what the underlying science, technology, and engineering have to offer, and to apply this knowledge to overall strategic planning. Indeed, to engender more respect for the technical side of business, business education may have to be reformed, or alternatives established to the conventional business schools, to create a new generation to be the counterparts of the Mercks, Noyces, and Lands of the older one. Promotion policies should give weight towards scientific expertise, so that there will be more CEOs with technical backgrounds. In short, we need the "rediscovery" by management of science.

Such a shift has implications for the universities. For it would mean many more university–industry partnerships, and industry support of university science totaling far more than the 5 percent we have today. Note that this shift in the structure and values of industry could occur *without* the universities. Or it could embrace them to the point of bringing about a new relationship like that between farmers and the old land-grant schools. But if the universities see industry's advance towards them as merely another chance for a handout, another prospective subsidy for basic-research-is-best, this new, more fruitful relationship will not come to pass.

First, companies should band together to help set research priorities, both for area universities and inter-company research institutes where appropriate. The healthy trend in New Jersey, North Carolina, and parts of California for clusters of companies using related technology fields to group together in a region, should continue. Such groupings probably improve each company's quality. They also give local academic institutions a focus for their applied science. While we are skeptical that all these budding regional partnerships will work—Silicon Valleys are not grown overnight, and there is more to creating the necessary inter-institutional synergism than meets the eye—nonetheless a concerted effort over the next 20 years could lead to a healthy number of such regional endeavors.

In addition, companies should consider borrowing bright young postdoctoral scientists for 1- or 2-year fellowship programs in industry before they return to their academic careers. By placing these select few well, by offering them tempting, intellectually challenging problems and good pay, the companies would benefit from the insights they provide and make them realize the importance of industrial needs. Such fellowships, described further below, could be the "hard" science equivalent of the M.D.-Ph.D. system that has been so effective for U.S. medicine.

3. Third, **the U.S. university science system should be reconfigured**. This is perhaps our most important recommendation. The postwar science system has spread basic research thinly around many institutions and has made university scientists working on applied problems unhappy. A greater concentration of basic science effort may be needed. Perhaps only the twenty top-ranked universities should remain striving for world-class basic science at the frontier. These institutions would do applied science as well, and would doubtless attract industrial support because of their quality. This is one of many ways that a consolidated and richer basic science system could expand its linkages to the larger fabric of societal needs.

We would bring about a value shift, however, to remove the tilt towards basic-science-is-best which has been overlaid on the universities for the past 30 years. For the main middle block of universities would continue some basic research, as overhead for their main work, which would be purposive basic science, applied science, and engineering. Thus, a mid-ranked university now struggling to keep up in math, chemistry, and physics would decide its physics department was its strongest basic research contribution, and focus on enhancing that nucleus of activity through investment of its "overhead" funding. Meanwhile, the mathematicians and chemists could stop tormenting themselves by playing the high-science game half way, and focus their research activity on other problems deemed most relevant to regional industrial priorities, the needs of the local workforce, and the need to provide the best training ground for students.

The motto of university science activities, we propose, should be to strive for excellent research at all costs, not basic research at any cost. Their focus should be science-for-society.

Finally, the universities in our reconfigured system could benefit from programs of industrial fellowships for postdocs mentioned above.

4. Fourth is a recommendation regarding professional values and the "ministry" of science Bush spoke of. In our view, this requires that **scientists and their students devote some part of their time, pro bono, to general education in the sciences**. They would run for school committees, help design curriculum materials, or organize local associations of faculty to work with the school superintendent or the local vocational schools. Many mechanisms are possible and the payoff can be large. What has been lacking is the professional will.

Much of the insecurity that has prompted scientific leaders to inflate the promises they make (promises of the "give us research funds and we will cure cancer" variety) stem from fears that the public does not understand science and, in a pinch, will stop supporting it. Weinberg's concept of science budgets as society's overhead, which we endorse, depends for its success upon enlightened public understanding of science. The profession could do much to make its long-term financial future more secure, therefore, by taking more responsibility for public education in the schools and popular media.

For example, scientists should forgive their colleagues who happen to be talented writers or are often on television. Popularization should be considered good and not something that detracts from the "real" work of science. Indeed, there should be more efforts like the Alfred P. Sloan Foundation's program of support to well-known scientists, such as physicist Freeman Dyson, to write their memoirs for general audiences.

5. A fifth point is the need for **an expanded commitment to internationalism, to the free flow of scientific information across national boundaries**. As pressures on them grow from domestic and international high-technology trade competition, U.S. scientists should counter with a concerted effort to reach out abroad.

A committee of the NSB has strongly endorsed such an effort,[6] but noted all the obstacles that make it vulnerable and may hinder the community from taking this obvious step: delays in the political system reaching decisions, threats to existing research budgets from new international programs, entanglements with foreign work that is of low priority, and loss of independence about directions and goals of U.S. projects. Our main proposal to overcome these hurdles would be our proposed advisory board, which could help the political system take decisions and guide relationships between international efforts and domestic science activity.

In any case, a commitment to internationalism is needed to maintain the quality of U.S. science, as foreign nations' scientific activity improves. Nonetheless, as we saw in Chapter 5, powerful social and economic pressures are keeping U.S. scientists, especially the younger ones who need foreign contacts most, at home.

A reversal of the isolationist trend of recent years could involve special federal government programs, new rules making a foreign trip easier on an ordinary grant, or even a new international initiative similar to the International Geophysical Year of 1957–1958 and the stream of international programs which followed. The NSB committee has also endorsed the possibility of such an effort.

6.   And what of basic research, that glittering diva who made her debut early in this essay? A notable feature of the story of postwar U.S. science, shown in Figure 1, was the very generosity of the taxpayers and politicians whose penny-pinching the postwar leaders of science feared. Today, while growth has slowed from the early days (and of course is not enough to pay for everything that the "free play" of pressures from scientists would like), it is growth nonetheless. Even the cuts in basic research feared when the Reagan administration first took office did not materialize. So there seems to be a genuine political consensus favoring basic research. Therefore, after 40 years, the high-science community should be mature and honest in the promises it makes.

Instead of arguing that it will cure our problems in energy, pollution, and so on, **scientists should agree that the sum spent on basic research is a tithe we all pay for being an enlightened society, an "overhead" on the whole enterprise.** Weinberg said it better:

> It is natural to propose that such basic research receive a certain fraction of the resources going into the applied research which it underlies. Every good applied research laboratory allocates to basic research a certain fraction of the resources allocated to it for its related applied research. . . . What I suggest is that on the na-

tional scale also, basic research be considered as a fixed charge on the applied research effort.

He then raised the argument (interesting to us) that society will pay this price only when it is so scientifically literate as to understand the true beauties of science, but rejected this as too Utopian a goal. So he concluded, it should be considered an

overhead charge on the society's entire technical enterprise — a burden that is assessed on the whole activity because, in a general and indirect sort of way, such basic science is expected eventually to contribute to the technological system as a whole.[7]

If we think of the basic research budget as overhead, and if we are explicit about the political consensus on its size, then scientists can stop being fixated with marginal changes in the yearly budget total and sort out their priorities within the request. How to spend it? Use it to support the elite groups who need additional funds for critical mass science. Use it to buy the best instrumentation and the best training at such institutions. Coordinate with other national programs to take most advantage of investments in science abroad. Send students on high-quality industry "internships" so that they will not forget society's needs in their future research careers. Copy Great Britain to the extent of being selective about the choices among fields.

And, by all means, fix up the procedures for running science so it can be fun again. There are many ways to do this, but we propose: (a) Agree within fields on which journals "count" as professionally excellent, and judge scientists by how useful their papers are, not how many they publish. Journals could continue to use peer reviewers in a limited, careful way. But only if the number of journals considered respectable is limited can scientific publishing become again the arbiter of who, and what work, is good. (b) Award funds on the basis of past performance and short proposals — not 100-page promises and manpower-intensive peer review. One of us has proposed a formula for performance evaluation elsewhere.[8] A group of researchers or a laboratory would receive funds on the basis of numbers of graduated students, and how many papers are published in journals that "count" (or, alternatively, the overall number of citations). Two other factors would measure how useful society thinks the group is: the funds received from federal mission agencies and the amount of industry support. In this way (or some other), any group's "overhead" could be calculated. (c) Finally, all awards should be long-term, perhaps 3 to 5 years, with an evaluation near the end to consider a renewal. Thus, by moving funds around in larger blocks, over longer periods, with less turbulence, the energies of many people — investigators, reviewers, grants administrators — could be freed and basic science would acquire more vigor.

As part of this reform, we would urge federal science agencies to encourage organizational innovation too, across disciplinary boundaries, or forming disciplinary mergers as fields change. If government research managers are willing to encourage such reforms, the universities will be encouraged to follow suit. Thus, besides being much simpler, the reformed scientific research system would be more flexible as well. Such changes would, naturally, require normative judgments and difficult choices, but, as Weinberg wrote, choices in science cannot, in the end, be avoided.

Gerald Holton has written: "for any professional activity has a just claim to moral authority when and only when it is widely seen to honor both truth and the public interest." For years, it seems, U.S. science has served the truth, but has served the public interest only intermittently.

All we propose is a redress of the balance, a return to the values Vannevar Bush himself wrote about and lived. Put another way, of the many, many problems science can address, those involving humanity itself, those that bear on its health and future well-being and the needs of the country are, at the moment, most important. Lewis Thomas seemed to say this in his 1981 Cosmos Club award lecture. He said that three fascinating studies could be done by modern science. Two were abstract: one dealt with honeybees, the other with music. But it was a third question, which held great promise for improving human health, that he regarded as urgent. He said[9]:

Some years ago, Dr. Harold Wolff, professor of neurology at Cornell, conducted the following experiment. He hypnotized some healthy volunteer subjects, and while they were under deep hypnosis he touched their forearms with an ordinary pencil which he told them was an extremely hot object; then he brought them out of the hypnotic state. In most cases, what happened was the prompt development of an area of redness and swelling at the skin site touched by the pencil, and in some subjects this went on to form a typical blister. I want to know all about that phenomenon. I want to know also how it happens that patients with intractable warts of long standing can have their warts instructed to drop off while under hypnosis.

Come to think of it, I would rather have a clear understanding of this phenomenon than anything else I can think of at the moment. The bees and the music can wait.

We like to think that Albert Einstein, too, shared the values we propose for a renewed, reconfigured, American science. In a 1934 talk he said[10]:

It is not enough that you should understand about applied science in order that your work may increase man's blessings. Concern for man himself and his fate must always form the chief interest of all technical endeavors, concern for the great unsolved problems of the organization of labor and the distribution of goods — in order that the creations of our minds shall be a blessing and not a curse to mankind. Never forget this in the midst of your diagrams and equations.

NOTES

[1] John Naisbitt, *Megatrends*, Warner Books, 1982, pp. 13, 14.

[2] *Ibid.*, p. 15, 16, 17.

[3] Alvin M. Weinberg, "Criteria for Scientific Choice," *Minerva*, Vol. 1, 1963, pp. 160, 171.

[4] Philip M. Smith, "The National Science Board and the Formulation of National Science Policy," National Science Foundation, NSB-81-440, 1981.

[5] Alvin M. Weinberg, "Criteria for Scientific Choice II: The Two Cultures," *Minerva*, Vol. 3, 1964, p. 6.

158   *Lost at the Frontier*

⁶ "Roles and Responsibilities of the National Science Foundation for Aspects of International Cooperation Related to the Health of American Science," Committee on International Science, National Science Board, May 1984, pp. 6, 19.

⁷ Weinberg, "Criteria for Scientific Choice II . . .," pp. 7, 8, 12.

⁸ Rustum Roy, "An Alternative Funding Mechanism," *Science*, Vol. 211, 27 March 1981, p. 1377, and "Alternative to Peer Review?" *Science*, Vol. 212, 19 June 1981, p. 1338.

⁹ Lewis Thomas, "Things Unflattened by Science," The Nineteenth Cosmos Club Award Lecture, Cosmos Club, Washington, D.C., 1982.

¹⁰ Albert Einstein, Caltech Talk, 1934.

Appendix
Invited Responses

ALTHOUGH sweeping, our essay cannot be comprehensive. Furthermore, the problems we raise and their causes and solutions have many possible interpretations. So we invited several people, either who were directly involved in the main events in our story or who have special expertise on aspects of it, to respond. Each was invited to write whatever he wished; disagreement was invited as well. We hope the resulting responses, which follow here, help crystallize some of the issues we raise. Again, we extend thanks to these contributors.

Response from • WILLIAM O. BAKER

William O. Baker joined Bell Telephone Laboratories in 1939 with degrees from Washington College and Princeton University. In 1948 he became head of Polymer Research and Development, in 1951 he became assistant director of Chemical and Metallurgical Research, and in 1955 he became vice president of the Laboratories for research. He was made president in 1973 and chairman of the board in 1979, from which position he retired in 1980. He has also served on the National Science Board and the National Cancer Advisory Board. He was the first member of all three academies: the National Academy of Sciences, the National Academy of Engineering, and the Institute of Medicine. He is the vice-chairman of the New Jersey Board of Higher Education and the chairman of the board of the Andrew W. Mellon Foundation.

Deborah Shapley and Rustum Roy's essay dramatizes the relations of discovery and innovation in science and engineering to the humanistic, sociopolitical, and economic concerns of our times. It illuminates the critical role of research and development laboratories which our industrial economy relies on for essential missions in agriculture, defense, energy, environment, transportation, and other public functions. My comment will describe four aspects of the operation of AT&T Bell Laboratories which are relevant to the authors' concerns: our use of new organizational groupings, our need to meet the particular requirements of scientific personnel, our need to define the scientific "expectations" arising from ongoing research, and, finally, the need to root technical operations in their scientific base. We will comment finally on the role of the university milieu for such research and development laboratories and how this milieu can help them pursue the twentieth-century American frontier.

Definitions of science and technology for an industrial economy are elusive. A simplistic view would say that industrial laboratories exist purely to enhance profits. More broadly, however, they offer nothing less than survival and renewed opportunity for the parent company. Let us look briefly at how the concerns of Shapley and Roy have been dealt with in the business of telecommunications and its electronic and photonic derivatives.

That business came from invention, mostly by Alexander Graham Bell. The telecommunications industry never had an independent resource base like oil or metals or farmland or steel. It had to generate a set of values which were not natural, like the nourishment of bread from grain or the strength of a steel bar or the speed with which a wheeled vehicle like an auto or railroad engine can provide for human motion. It had to deal with the intangibles and subtleties of human communication by voice and vision, and later with the even more unfamiliar expression of numbers and data. This was all done by encoding or otherwise re-expressing human language, itself already an elaborate and complex coding system facilitating thought and action.

This "artificial" value system meant that there had to be a constant search for basic units. Otherwise the engineering of telephony and even telegraphy would vary from language to language and from one medium of transmission to another. So early on, electromagnetic theory and acoustic principles, both intrinsic to the coding and processing of telephony, telegraphy, video, and their derivatives, became the engineering and scientific context for our business.

The rest of the story is widely known and is well illustrated in the main essay in this volume. We soon found in electrical communications what physiologists such as Harvey had found out about living things, namely, that there is a system which interconnects all parts and on which all input and output functions depend. In the case of telecommunications, this system, expressed by electromagnetic theory and other fundamental ideas, drove succeeding generations of scientific leaders and administrators of our laboratories to organize science and engineering as a *systems continuum*, joining basic research to applications and engineering.

This *systems continuum* stimulated the invention of systems engineering with Bell Laboratories by George Gilman and his associates. Systems development, intrinsic to the telecommunications business (at least before its recent forced disintegration), is also basic to other industrial innovation. For as industrial technology becomes the more sophisticated, the less people are impressed by changes of components in a given system, be it transport, health care, food production, entertainment, or communications. Rather, they perceive significant change only when the total system changes. In telecommunications, for example, the substitution of transistors for vacuum tubes in radios and television sets aroused little interest until the whole receiving system was drastically altered by the great reductions in power used, through small batteries, higher reliability, and enhanced performance. Similarly, in the automobile industry, ongoing elegant changes in gasoline octane for fuels has no significant impact until corresponding changes in engine cost, weight, acceleration and durability convince the buyer that the automotive transport system has been improved.

As for our research and development activities, this circumstance requires and stimulates the continuous conversion of basic new knowledge into applications and engineering. It leads to interdisciplinary effort on the creativity end, and to versatile engineering and technology on the production end. In our postwar effort in telecommunications, the expression in basic scientific terms of systems advances has led to the anticipation of new components such as transistors, lasers, thin film circuits, isolators, gyrators, and others, and to new ways of putting these together into new systems guided by new scientific principles.

Within our Laboratories, all of this meant studying and attempting to express and structure modern science and technology. We had to face every facet of the transitions and application of discovery under the tight rein of economic viability and consumer acceptance.

In order to extend the basis of new knowledge, we had to generate organizational groupings heretofore untried in industry. In the 1950s, for example, we established a department of theoretical physics, a center of computer science, a laboratory of behavioral research and human factors, and later an economics research center. We established a division for operations research and quality assurance, binding heretofore unconnected aptitudes; in it, that now-sacred commercial resource, quality control, was born and reared.

With respect to this art of applying science, discussed so well in the opening pages of Shapley and Roy's essay, we have in Bell Laboratories a long and vivid tradition of field operations, close and interesting association among engineers and scientists through the medium of materials science and engineering. Matter, after all, is the common denominator ranging from solid state physics theory to outside plant engineering (in which wires and poles have to sustain ice storms, tornados, sunshine, and hydration). One of the organizational tactics supporting the general thesis in this essay is that materials research and development have been kept together in a single major division of the laboratories since the 1950s, whereas nearly every other program has had separate, although complementary, research and developmental divisions.

The Laboratories' circumstances of invention raised *expectations* for what still more invention and discovery could reveal. Already, communications had demonstrated startling revisions of the human concepts of space and time, just as the wheel must have at its initiation. So we had an ingredient for economic and social advance, to which the laboratory worker could apply huge expectations. We developed an "expectations tactic" that explored the whole concept of what ongoing science and technology done in the Laboratories could do in the next stages, and what is possible and probable in research and development. Whereas systems engineering aided in determining the full range of our requirements, this expectations tactic examined the full range of scientific possibilities before us and served as a technical basis for action.

This expectations tactic (a term unique to our Laboratories) has been applied especially in the domains of materials and information and communications. It facilitated a convergence of the ways of organizing and using new knowledge, aided by computers, automata, and telecommunications, with systematic science and engineering in the field of solid state physics.

Expectations properly expressed indeed provide a motive for research effort and originality of the highest quality. But they have to be phrased in appropriately credible form, for which the broad fabric of systems engineering is suitable. In our laboratories' initiation of solid state and semiconductor research objectives that led to the transistor, for example, the reference point was the amplifying system of vacuum tubes but also vacuum electronics in global telephony through cables and radio. Systems engineering led us to hope that if only a few things could be done to Joe Becker's diodes and thermistors used in the vacuum devices, the communications system would be enhanced. These concerns helped guide William Shockley's afternoon and evening seminars before World War II, where, at a very fundamental scientific level, we sought to relate E. Wilson's and John Clarke Slater's and Eugene Wigner's insights into crystals and semiconductors to the electronic possibilities.

Likewise in the late 1950s, when millimeter wavelengths were seen as revolutionary in themselves (we were already exploiting them for waveguide), we recognized that the millimeter portion of the spectrum was not big enough to accommodate future communications needs. Our expectations tactic led us to explore other parts of the spectrum, at faster frequencies, where we suspected Nature had hidden away important secrets. We eagerly welcomed the optical frequency concepts of Arthur Schawlow and Charles Townes, following Townes' spectroscopy at microwave frequencies and the maser. Their discovery of the laser and the 1958 patent and publications thus came into a warmly hospitable climate of communications hopes and expectations.

This era from the 1950s to the 1980s was also characterized by the notion that the fundamental physics of atoms, molecules, and crystals, along with the chemistry of their purity and processing, would vastly enlarge the spectrum of expectations built around the concepts of information coding and transfer of Harry Nyquist and Ralph V. L. Hartley. These concepts were recast by Claude Shannon's historic principle of information and communications theory. Particularly, the universality of digital encoding was combined with the bistable (hence binary) conditions of basic physics (i.e., that electric charges are positive-or-negative, magnetic poles are north-or-south, energy transitions are on-or-off, etc.).

The Shannon theorem illustrates another essential aspect in the organization of productive industrial science and engineering. This is the need for *guiding principles which link the function of the system to its scientific base*, even beyond the operational elements. Thus, when George Stibitz conceived the electrical digital computer and built one out of telephone relays, he already knew Boolean algebra and John von Neumann's ideas of logic and memory. Because of this knowledge, he was able to synthesize brilliantly an electromechanical device array, operating with contacts and magnetic fields, into a computer. Without this knowledge, the nature of the functioning of the future machine would have remained obscure, and only an incremental improvement on simple switching machines would have resulted. Today, the same tactics and organizing principles are illustrated in carrier systems multiplexing, electronic switching, radio relay including satellites, and now photonics and lightguides, with the Integrated Digital Services Network being created from them.

Embedded throughout the whole exercise of research, exploratory and applied development, and engineering is the single creative human brain, the unit from which all such progress ensues. Thus, special efforts have been made to enhance individual initiatives by the tens of thousands of persons, representing both new talent and experienced skills, with whom we have been privileged to be associated in the Laboratories. These have included frequent seminars and individually generated technical memoranda through which the scientist, engineer, technologist, or aide can, any time, communicate a finding or propose an idea. Likewise, publication, attending international conferences, and other forms of recognition have accented the role of the individual in a community so large that there might have been a temptation for submergence. Our primary concern for a quarter century included assuring suitable personal environs and aims for the brilliant discoverers of the silicon solar cell, charge coupled devices, hard superconducting magnets, the optical system defying the Boltzmann law that came to be called the laser, satellite communications, photonic circuitry, computer operating languages like C, and systems like Unix.

Thus we have reflected on some of the organizational policy issues central to Shapley and Roy's insightful critique of the balance among basic research, applied research, technology, and engineering in our nation. We conclude that the large and relatively autonomous research and development enterprises are where fundamental new knowledge, acquired with intellectual challenge similar to university conditions, can be transferred efficiently to applied science, which then supports development and engineering of products and services.

Such organizations require the intellectual milieu of the university as well. In the case of our experience at Bell Laboratories, the major role of the universities has been to identify and develop the best of human talent. Now in order to train that talent, universities need to do research, and it is essential that the quality of university research be good, whether of the frontier variety or not. One way to improve the role of universities in our national endeavors could be to focus on their role as educators, for which a very high quality of research activity is essential, whether it be "basic" science or not. There has been on the part of some universities an illusion of high creativity and scientific frontiersmanship. But if universities adjusted realistically their research activities to this learning exercise, a wholly different research configuration would emerge.

As for research done by other industries beyond our own in telecommunications, systems engineering is a key administrative guide. But it requires special scientific credibility though describing fundamental physical, chemical, mathematical, and conceptual features such as telecommunications and computers have long had. These qualities are gaining in importance in automotive vehicles, aircraft, certain weapons systems, and energy distribution networks as well as in nuclear reactors. A particular challenge for the future will be with the establishment of similar systems of reference for biochemical and medical enterprises.

Response from • **GEORGE E. BROWN, JR.**

George E. Brown, Jr., is the long-time Democratic representative in Congress from the Riverside-San Bernardino area of Southern California. His long tenure in the Congress (1962–1970 and 1972 to present) and background as an industrial physicist have earned him a special role as a prominent scientist in Congress. As senior member of the House Science and Technology Committee, he is responsible for a number of initiatives to aid science and the formulation of national policy for science and technology, including proposals to create a National Technology Foundation parallel to the National Science Foundation.

Lost at the Frontier is a valuable contribution to the emerging and much-needed debate on U.S. policy for science and technology. Through my experience as a member of the House Committee on Science and Technology and as a layperson interested in science and technology, I have reached many of the same conclusions expressed here so forcefully by Deborah Shapley and Rustum Roy. I hope that the provocative ideas contained in this book will spark discussion and controversy and will lead to new policy directions. This book will be especially useful if it is widely read and debated, not only by the small circle of people who make up the science policy community, but also by the larger community of practicing scientists and engineers and by the general public.

One of the pleasures, as well as frustrations, of serving in Congress is seeing the linkages, or potential linkages, between the different sectors of society. In a healthy, dynamic society, those linkages are strong, thereby ensuring constant communication and interaction. When those linkages become strained or severed, the health of society suffers. This is precisely the problem that has arisen with U.S. science and technology. Important linkages between basic scientific research and other activities of our society have been allowed to atrophy. The goal of a new policy for science

168

and technology must be to re-establish those key bridges — between basic and applied research and between science and the goals of society.

The House Science and Technology Committee, in its annual review of the National Science Foundation's programs and budget, has tried to encourage the development of these linkages. For example, in our 1979 report on the NSF budget, we said:

> The Committee emphasizes its intent that the coupling of basic and applied research, and basic research and science educational functions be made as close, natural, and spontaneous as possible.[1]

But Congress has not always been successful in translating these words and intentions into positive action. Current funding constraints, pressure created by the decline of American technological preeminence in the international marketplace, and the debate over the appropriate roles of the public and private sectors have combined to force Congress to take a closer look at U.S. science and technology policy. Efforts to modify and, hopefully, improve that policy can be expected from Congress.

Basic Research, Applied Research, and Societal Needs

In some academic circles, basic research is known as *"pure research,"* a very revealing phrase. Of course, science is, and should be, pursued for "pure" reasons, such as intellectual curiosity; the aesthetic beauty of simple, elegant explanations of complex phenomena; and the satisfaction that comes from a greater understanding of nature. Nevertheless, as a useful exercise in understanding a public concern about basic research, to which a Congressman must respond frequently, the reader might try answering the following letter that I received from a constituent. The writer is complaining about a National Science Foundation grant given for entomological research:

> Here we go again, spending our money that *should* go to the needy. . . . This money that's being wasted could certainly help the folks in the unemployment line and also the coal mining towns. Why doesn't the government look at our own country and see the need instead of wasting it on studying bugs?

But basic research is also conducted within the larger context of society's needs and pursued for less "pure" reasons, such as the elimination of mindless labor, disease, hunger, and war. This link between fundamental scientific knowledge and societal needs is applied research. As Vannevar Bush's quotations in this book clearly illustrate, many scientists are well aware of the importance of applied research. Members of Congress, entrusted with the job of allocating federal expenditures to meet societal needs, have also stressed the importance of acquiring scientific knowledge for the purpose of improving our world. In a recent report of the House Science and Technology Committee, it was put this way:

> Applied research is a necessary and valuable portion of the programs of the National Science Foundation. Neither persistent demands for "relevance" nor a reactionary reverence for "purity" should interfere with a sound program balance between the advancement of knowledge desired for its contribution to science and the vigorous pursuit of knowledge desired for an application in filling human needs.[2]

Fortunately, successful counterexamples exist to Shapley and Roy's conclusion that in general U.S. science and industry are suffering from an imbalance between basic and applied research. Examples of strong linkages maintained between basic research and product development include Bell Laboratories, the agriculture research and extension system, and parts of the Department of Defense. We can also look abroad, particularly to Japan, for examples of success. It is, in fact, this foreign success in international trade that has finally attracted the attention of Congress to possible shortcomings in U.S. policy for science and technology.

But these examples of successful U.S. organizations are, unfortunately, often exceptions to the rule. For this reason, Congress is grappling with ways of developing linkages between basic and applied research like the ones found in the examples cited above. As discussed in the final chapter of *Lost at the Frontier*, one alternative I have proposed is the establishment of a National Technology Foundation as a way of consolidating and strengthening the generic aspects of technology-related programs which are currently scattered throughout the federal government.[3] This past year has seen a number of other proposals brought to light which share the common goal of establishing better linkages between basic and applied research in support of innovation and productivity. This includes a modest proposal of my own which would establish a separate engineering directorate at the National Science Foundation, the fate of which hangs in the balance as this goes to press. Without a coherent and vigorous federal policy of technology development and promotion, particularly in high-priority areas, the United States will not be able to compete effectively in future world trade, regardless of the mechanism used to accomplish this goal.

Science, Technology, and Strategic Visions

The strong link between science and societal goals is one of the fundamental reasons for recent Japanese economic success. The Japanese have developed an elaborate iterative process for bringing together representatives from various sectors of society to discuss, debate, refine, and finally agree on long-term goals. These "visions for the future" serve to channel the energy, enthusiasm, and creativity of the Japanese people, thus giving them an advantage over a society which does not generally like to set national priorities or societal needs.

A national consensus may be more difficult to reach in the United States because of our great diversity. Nevertheless, we must develop ways to engage in long-term strategic policy planning. Like any successful organization, our society needs a "strategic vision" for the future. Scientists must see themselves as an important part of the political process, and should not shy away from public service. It will take all of the best minds in many fields to develop a consensus for long-term strategic planning.

If the link between science and the goals of our society is strong and dynamic, the links between basic and applied research and between research and education will follow naturally from it. Vannevar Bush understood the need to work together for common goals when he wrote, "It [Science] can be effective in the national welfare only as a member of a team."[3] This crucial theme was even more vividly expressed by Henry Wallace, then the Secretary of Agriculture, in 1934:

> It is difficult to see how the engineer and the scientist can much longer preserve a complete isolation from the economic and social world around them. A world motivated by economic individualism has repeatedly come to the edge of the abyss, and this last time possibly came within a hair's breadth of plunging over. Yet science, all this time, has been creating another world and another civilization that simply must be motivated by some conscious social purpose, if civilization is to endure. Science and engineering will destroy themselves and the civilization of which they are a part unless there is built up a consciousness which is as real and definite in meeting social problems as the engineer displays when he builds his bridge.[4]

By strengthening the linkage between basic scientific research and other activities in our society, I believe that U.S. science and technology can be rescued and restored to its proper position of scouting "the endless frontier" and helping lead humanity forward into it.

NOTES

[1] Report to accompany H.R. 7115, Authorizing Appropriations to the National Science Foundation. From the Committee on Science and Technology, 16 May 1980, 96th Congress, 2nd Session, Report No. 96-999.

[2] Report to accompany H.R. 2729, Authorizing Appropriations to the National Science Foundation. From the Committee on Science and Technology, 21 March 1979, 96th Congress, 1st Session, Report 96-61.

[3] Vannevar Bush, *Science—The Endless Frontier*, p. 11.

[4] Henry A. Wallace, "The Social Advantages and Disadvantages of the Engineering–Scientific Approach to Civilization," *Science* (1934), Vol. 79, pp. 1–5.

Response from • PAT CHOATE

Pat Choate is senior policy analyst for TRW, Inc., and the coauthor of *America in Ruins, the Decaying Infrastructure* (with Susan Walter), *Being Number One, Rebuilding the U.S. Economy* (with Gail Schwartz), and *Thinking Strategically, a Primer for Public Leaders* (with Susan Walter). He has served on an NSF advisory panel on vocational education and training, as a member of the board of directors of 70,001 – The Youth Training Company, and as a member of the Advisory Board of the Clark Foundation. He has also held a variety of policy and administrative positions with the U.S. Department of Commerce and the state governments of Tennessee and Oklahoma. He often testifies to Congress on economic competitiveness, education and training, and management.

From time to time, a book, such as *The Other America, The Affluent Society*, or *The Silent Spring*, heightens the public's awareness and shapes its perception about a topic of vital concern. *Lost at the Frontier* is such a book.

Deborah Shapley and Rustum Roy advance a straightforward thesis: that is, U.S. scientists have unwittingly stumbled into a Faustian bargain with the federal government. As they have secured generous federal funding for their work, their linkages with society have been weakened and their role has been diluted.

In their search for federal funding, scientists have devolved into just another special interest group pleading for more funds and another supplicant at the door of federal agencies seeking another grant. In the process, scientists have lost much of their former influence as advisors to the public, business, and government. They have also permitted their work to be shaped by the vagaries of federal political fashion, the stop-start timing of federal appropriations, and the red tape of the federal bureaucracy.

Perhaps the most insidious damage done by this Faustian bargain results from the false values it creates – the perception that successful scientists publish widely, that research work in a university is more prestigious than research in industry, and that

173

science is more important than engineering. One of the consequences is predictable: a frayed relationship between science and business.

As the authors point out, scientists once worked closely with industry. As they solved problems essential to the development and introduction of products, industry reciprocated with funding and interaction. Agricultural research is the classic example of the benefits of linking basic research to the needs of users, the farmers. As much as a quarter of most farmers' time is devoted to experimentation of various sorts, often in close cooperation with county agents and technicians who help bring scientific advances out of the laboratory and into the marketplace. The authors point out that such approaches continue to underpin some industries such as the new biotechnology companies, and have been normal in some firms such as the Bell Laboratories. But they also note that such linkages are far from the norm.

As the links between science and business have been broken, both parties have suffered. Scientists have lost the independence that comes from having support from multiple sectors. They have lost much of the discipline created by the need of business to be relevant. At the same time, the capacity of business to innovate has been diminished.

The broken linkages between basic science, engineering, and commercial applications also reinforce the increased emphasis of U.S. business on short-term performance and investment in a vicious cycle. As science has been mystified and isolated, business has become less willing to gamble on basic research whose eventual relevance is uncertain. The National Science Board's *Science Indicators 1976*, for instance, found that over the past three decades, improvements in U.S. technology have increasingly shifted from fundamental breakthroughs, such as the creation of the transistor, to refinements in existing technologies. The harm done to U.S. competitiveness is obvious: the slowed introduction of better production techniques and more innovative products reduces both U.S. productivity and the attractiveness of U.S. products and services.

Finally, the dependence of scientists on federal funding and their isolation from the challenges of the larger society have

weakened their linkages with state governments. This is fatal to
U.S. science since much of the nation's basic research is conducted
in state universities. A growing number of reports document that
in these key institutions, university equipment and facilities are
limited and faculty salaries are not competitive.

Although these deficiencies are known, the states are not taking action because those who provide the required funds —
governors and legislators — fail to see that the work of their
university scientists is more relevant than competing uses of those
public funds. The scientists have done little to help their university
spokesmen argue successfully on their behalf. Nor have they been
enthusiastic participants in efforts that demonstrate the value of
greater investment by state governments.

Some states, such as Tennessee and Oklahoma, have attempted
to make the connection between science in their universities and
state businesses. Their success has been limited. In significant
part, this is because the scientists had little interest, motivation,
incentive, or understanding of the needs of business. These experiments suggest that strengthening the linkages between science
and business cannot be done quickly or on an ad hoc basis.
Rather, they must be a natural, ongoing part of a spectrum of
activities — research, engineering, and application.

What this book makes clear is that neither the nation nor
science can afford the isolation of science from society. It offers
some practical steps that can be taken. But its greatest contribution is its "emperor has no clothes" message. And that awareness
is the first and most important step in reuniting science with
society.

Harry C. Gatos is professor of Electronic Materials and Professor of Molecular Engineering at M.I.T. He graduated in chemistry from the University of Athens in 1945 and came to the United States. He was a research engineer at Du Pont, 1952–1955, and then joined M.I.T.'s Lincoln Laboratory, rising to become head of its Solid State Division in 1964. In 1962 he assumed his two professorships at the Institute. As a leading university scientist working at the cutting edge of the electronics revolution, he has earned several awards, among them NASA's Award for Outstanding Scientific Achievement.

This is a timely, exceedingly thoughtful and thought-provoking essay. Its outstanding feature is that it convincingly traces problems to their roots and critically addresses cause and effect relationships. By demonstrating the indispensable interdependence of research, development, and production in making a technological impact, it paints a more realistic picture of today's role of science than that which is in the minds of most educators, industrial planners, and government strategists.

My comments stem from my long career as a working scientist striving through advances in science, and through education, to impact technology. I will limit these comments to the field of electronic materials and their applications since that is the field I am most familiar with.

My first position outside a university was in the research laboratories of a large chemical company in the early 1950s. Research was highly thought of there but I was rather disappointed in a few years: communication between research and production was essentially nonexistent. The excitement associated with the relevance of the research findings to technology was missing. Especially because the chemical industry was mature, it did not quite feel right.

176

A strong reason for my joining the Lincoln Laboratory of M.I.T. in 1955 was the prevailing strong interplay there between basic research and applications (and among disciplines). Here is one example (of many) of this type of interplay. A physicist gave us some specifications of a material in a single crystal form which would be suitable for the fabrication of a three-level maser. After a few false starts the host crystal and the paramagnetic dopant were identified (cobalticyanide containing chromium ions). Within days after the first crystal was grown, the first three-level solid state maser was operating. Within months, the maser, a solid state amplifier, was incorporated into a radar system and was successfully used to accurately measure for the first time the distance between Venus and Earth. This was the beginning of our ability to accurately measure distances between stars.

In my reports on my trips to the Soviet Union in the 1960s, I pointed out that that country was ahead of us in my field of electronic materials and specifically semiconductors. One of the obvious reasons was that it had many more scientists available for and engaged in research than we did. Entire research institutes were dedicated to individual semiconductors (there were separate ones for silicon, silicon carbide, and III-V compounds). My industrial friends in the United States did not quite agree with me, pointing out that our electronic materials components and systems were far more advanced than those in the Soviet Union. On the other hand, my friends in government agreed but were not concerned: they pointed out that the interfaces between research and development, and development and production, in the Soviet Union were not working well at all. I agreed with this point: obviously, those interfaces bridging research, development, and production were working better in this country at that time than in the Soviet Union or anywhere else, for that matter.

Although it is not possible to assess quantitatively all the factors that contributed to the golden years of the 1960s for research, development, and advanced technology, certain critical elements are rather clear. Research (basic and applied) occupied a very prestigious position in industry and in the government. Research and development funds were unlimited, it seems. Advanced technologies based on solid state electronics were becoming financial successes very rapidly. Research, development, and production were feeding on one another.

It was in the 1960s that the interdisciplinary Materials Research Laboratories were founded and funded in thirteen universities by the Department of Defense's Advanced Research Projects Agency. They made possible teaching and research in new areas. It was through M.I.T.'s MRL that I started my Electronic Materials group. I often daydream of the equipment and research facility funds that were made available to me during the first few years of my group's existence. Such resources don't exist anymore.

Today in semiconductor materials and applications Japan has an imposing lead. The quality of silicon crystals produced by Japanese companies is superior to that produced by domestic companies. Furthermore, processes involved in chip fabrication are under better control in Japan than in this country. In the rapidly developing gallium arsenide optoelectronics, Japan has pulled way ahead. Sumitomo Electric produces superior gallium arsenide crystals compared to those in this country. In fact it now sells 75 percent of the gallium arsenide sold in the free world. In gallium arsenide devices and integrated circuits, the situation is similar. This increasing technological gap between Japan and this country is alarming.

What happened to this country? The answer lies in this book's main theme: the interplay among research, development, and production deteriorated. In industry, with minor exceptions, the time-span of research and development goals was reduced to about 3 years. Critical areas of electronic materials research were dropped. Research on crystal growth from the melt became nonexistent.

The U.S. electronics revolution of the 1960s was made possible by a generation of chips with a number of discrete devices on the order of 1,000 on a surface about 3 × 3 mm in size. Greater densities of devices were limited by inhomogeneities in the crystals grown from molten silicon. In 1970, we announced in the open literature that the use of magnetic fields virtually eliminates the convection in molten silicon which creates these inhomogeneities, thereby explaining how a new generation of silicon crystals of greater purity could be grown. I discussed these findings with many of my American industrial friends; I was just given a courteous ear. But Sony of Japan picked up my results; a few years later it applied these laboratory findings to commercial production of silicon chips. The Japanese thus acquired an edge in the new generation of chips with a number of discrete devices on the order of 100,000 per 3 × 3 mm chip and produced them in commercially viable yields from very pure crystals.

The U.S. government agencies failed to identify the important areas of semiconductor materials research and did not recognize what was happening in the 1970s. In the late 1970s, I was told that gallium arsenide would never amount to anything of practical importance. I was also told by a government agency that silicon was a mature technology and there was no need for further research on it. Yet today, driven by Japan's advances, a new electronics revolution has been launched based in fiber optics technology relying on gallium arsenide optoelectronics and chips with circuit speeds promising to be 10 to 100 times the speed of silicon, heralding a new era in electronics, new even to computer experts.

Even now in the United States, no master plan, not even a plan, has been visible to me which related the emerging technological needs in electronic materials to relevant and appropriate research and development programs.

In the universities, research and teaching on semiconductor materials began to be fashionable only in the last 2 to 3 years.

The Japanese government has played a major role in identifying critical areas of semiconductor research and development and co-sponsoring programs on them through industrial and university consortia.

Any intimate interplay developed in the 1960s among industry, government, and university on solid state electronics seems to have been lost in the 1970s. Speaking for myself, in the 1960s, I was constantly being made aware by my industrial colleagues of the critical technical issues that needed to be addressed; this awareness helped me orient my students and their research towards realistic problems. The government agencies too were concerned with specific problems but sought their solution on a broad basis that included research, development and education. There may be no simple prescription as to how to pursue the "endless frontiers" of science. It is perfectly clear, however, that close interplay among government, industry, and university enhances the working efficiency of the interfaces among research, development, and production.

Response from • **WALTER A. HAHN**

Walter A. Hahn is Futurist-in-Residence and Visiting Professor of Business and Government, George Washington University. He was from 1972–1982 Senior Specialist in Science, Technology and Futures Research of the Congressional Research Service. Previously, he was at General Electric as a business operations researcher and systems engineer. He has served as Director of Management Analysis for NASA (1961–1962), as Deputy Assistant Secretary of Commerce for Science and Technology Planning (1969–1970), on the White House's national goals staff (1970), and as Director of Policy Analysis for the Department of Commerce (1971).

The changes occurring in the environment of U.S. science and technology and within science itself are more far-reaching and profound than Shapley and Roy indicate. I would fault this otherwise commendable essay for dwelling too much on the past and the problems of today at the expense of the future. For there is a critical need for what I will call the S&T community — which includes engineers and technologists and analysts, not just university basic scientists — to devise new institutions and take advantage of modern futures and foresight methods in order to be viable in the future. The U.S. S&T community, however exquisitely scientifically literate, needs to overcome its hidebound social and political *il*literacy to deal with the new realities around it. I propose that we, in the S&T community, network our way towards self-reform and a viable future.

Disagreements with Shapley and Roy

The authors note that their essay is "an experiment in science criticism" and is neither "scientific" *per se* nor to be judged by "scientific" standards. I share their concern that this latter point may be unacceptable to their readers, particularly the scientists.

181

Nonetheless, the discussion of the problems of science can no longer be restricted to the scientists' favorite methodologies, for the large-scale and central role of science and technology in modern society mean they are too important to be left to the scientists. Science and technology are society's business.

The tree metaphors are another problem. Shapley and Roy argue that the widely accepted "single tree" metaphor for the relationship between basic science and technology is "wrong." Rather than a single tree whose roots are watered by support of undirected basic research and whose fruits are technology (water the tree and both grow), they prefer one technology tree and a second basic science tree. Their claim that these two metaphorical trees are separate but linked does not fit either my experience or some of their own arguments and those of Derek deSolla Price which they cite. (On the other hand, the single tree model is widely believed and has lots of our initials carved on it! So perhaps its fallacies are worth some discussion!) In my own work I have found a simple open-system model most useful: science feeds technology; technology feeds science; and all kinds of environmental factors influence in both positive and negative, and sometimes unknown, ways. But I suggest that readers not be distracted by which model is right (if any). None are central to the authors' main proposition that improvement is needed in the internal workings of science and its contributions to society.

The authors praise the continuing linkage of basic and applied science in some areas of national defense. They should have named the Mansfield Amendment which cut the links between basic and applied defense research by prohibiting the Department of Defense (DOD) from funding any basic research having no military use. Although the amendment legally expired with the appropriations bill to which it was attached, the hangover effects of the cutoff were perpetuated for years by the bureaucracy, including that of agencies outside the DOD. Only in the last few years have its debilitating effects in cutting these linkages been wiped out (almost).

Finally, Shapley and Roy argue that scientists are hindered by their need to be "scientific" about policy issues. And if, as they also argue, scientists should be more responsive to society's needs, they must be equally responsible for the social, economic, environmental, and even political impacts of their contributions. Although there is an emerging area, risk assessment, which would help to do this, unfortunately the main thrust of this new field is coming from outside the S&T community. Some scientists are trying to make risk assessment thoroughly "scientific" by elaborate methodologies that stress logic over reality, but here too, scientists should be wary of being too "scientific" and indulging in pseudoscience.

In contrast, I agree with a major point: the authors' argument that society should be the business of science. The authors perform a service in exploring the state of our system for producing science and technology and in suggesting a "new contract" between science and society. I support their six conclusions and five of their proposals in their last chapter. But I would change some of their priorities and wording. Their first proposal for an "independent advisory board . . . with some authority" is both self-contradictory and will not achieve the authors' stated goals. If it is only "advisory," it will have no authority; if it does have "authority," it will be able to act unilaterally and will disregard the consensus among all parties to the science-and-society contract that we all agree is needed.

The Need for Foresight

Assume for the moment that the authors' propositions are realized and we value equally applied and basic research, interconnect them, and create an ideal climate for all three types of research — undirected, purposive, and applied. Will U.S. science and society be happy with each other in another 30 years — e.g., in 2015? Now is the time to think about it, to exercise foresight. We should have done it long ago.

In recent years there have been the beginnings of a futures orientation in science and technology policy. The technology assessment thrust of the late 1960s and early 1970s produced much publicity, many reports, and a new institution for Congress, the Office of Technology Assessment (OTA). But these have yet to fulfill their promise: probably the requirement for federal environmental impact statements of all federal projects required by the National Environmental Policy Act of 1970 has had more effect in forcing the government to think ahead than has OTA.

In the early 1970s, the House of Representatives altered its rules (Rule X, General Oversight Provision) to state:

> Each standing committee other than budget and appropriations . . . shall on a continuing basis undertake futures research and forecasting on matters within the jurisdiction of that committee.

As a result, some committees and subcommittees have held foresight hearings on energy, aging, small business, and other topics. The 1976 National Science and Technology Policy, Organization and Priorities Act in Section 206 provided for a 5-year outlook study, but compromises in the bill's language left the function vulnerable to the near-extinction it is now approaching.[1]

But overall, the track record for foresight and assessment in national science and technology activities is one of hesitating starts and no finishes. We need to institutionalize looking through the windshield instead of in the rearview mirror, if we are to avoid the mistakes and missed opportunities Shapley and Roy say happened in the implementation of the Bush report.

The Need for New Institutions and Paradigms

Shapley and Roy point out, I think correctly, that throwing more money at today's research and development establishment will not solve the problems of (1) a perceived decline in basic and applied science productivity and relevance and (2) revitalizing U.S. technology to meet future domestic and foreign trade needs. I agree that a shift of values is necessary, but it is not sufficient.

We need organizational innovation also. Historically we invented a variety of institutional forms in response to socioeconomic and other needs. An early institutional invention, the corporation, was the basis for the later, hierarchical "scientifically" managed company. For other purposes, we invented nonprofit corporations and government corporations like Comsat. Universities use very old organizational innovations: discipline-based departments grouped into colleges, schools, and centers.

Matrix management was the brainchild of industrial managers, uncertain whether to organize around their products, processes, location of supplies, or customers.

Now, all around us we see new needs and changing environments: international technological competition, domestic and global economic malaise, changed values and lifestyles, changed demography, and the transition from a "things" to an "information and services" society.

So not only do we need to reform and revitalize many of our institutions, not only research institutions, but we need to invent new ones.[2] A major area of reform could come from taking a "hard science" research laboratory approach to "soft science" issues. Look at the new individualistic organization of development of computer software, or even Lockheed's creative "Skunkworks" where many of the best aircraft were built. Why can't we adopt this "hard science" model to our institutional needs? Why not establish laboratories for research and development organization innovation? Why not experiment with organizations themselves?

We in the S&T community need to change the lenses in the glasses through which we look at our S&T enterprise. Much recent research has concluded that science is becoming more holistic. Most of us were raised with Thomas Kuhn's famous paradigm for science. But Fritjof Capra's recent book, *The Turning Point: Science, Society, and the Rising Culture* (Simon and Schuster, 1982), emphasizes our "crisis of perception" in applying a dated Cartesian-Newtonian worldview of today's reality. The transition to a holistic view of science was described in a key Congressional document thus[3]:

> The objective and deterministic, or cause and effect, approaches to science that have evolved over the last three hundred years are increasingly being perceived as insufficient for the solution of social, technological, environmental, economic, and political problems. Holistic and systemic features which are based on overall relationships are increasingly entering many fields of science. In parallel, subjective features and an increasing emphasis on individual and social developments are of direct concern. Values and goal-oriented activities are part of, not apart from, the solution of problems. Research and applications in the contextual and prob-

lem-oriented policy sciences complement the traditional, basic, discipline-oriented physical and biological sciences of the past. . . .

However, the document went on to recognize that scientists, locked in their Cartesian-Newtonian boxes, are the most likely to resist this change. It continued:

> Like all transitions, those in them have the hardest time observing changes. And the stake holders — in this case, successful reductionist scientists and engineers who believe that the nature of reality can be understood by comprehending the nature of its constituent parts — will deny the change and fight desperately to retain the status quo. It may be a case when an understanding but nonscientist view of the transition . . . may be applied to great advantage.

Parallel shifts in view are occurring in economics and other fields.[4]

A Program for Change

Marshalling the will and resources to bring about major social, institutional, and resource allocation changes is extraordinarily difficult in our society. The constraints of our system prevent change by fiat, and we want those constraints to remain, obviously. Fortunately, our system allows each of us to initiate change. Each of us can do something, but none of us can force the other to change to our "right" way.

Among our obstacles are three illiteracies. First is the much-discussed technological illiteracy on the part of the public, politicians, managers, lawyers, and economists in particular. The second illiteracy is the scientists' political and social illiteracy. They often don't know how, or want, to proceed in any manner other than "scientifically." For all of its power in wresting secrets from nature and stimulating creative genius, science is a wimp when faced with irrationality, high emotion, admitted bias, committed self-interest, ignorance, apathy, and dozens of other human and societal attributes. The problems facing the conduct of science discussed by Shapley and Roy are not scientific problems amenable to scientific solutions. Thus, getting scientists to recognize that the solutions lie on the other guy's turf, the turf on which they are wimps, may be the biggest hurdle of all.

Our third illiteracy is cultural. Relatively speaking, only a small fraction of the U.S. S&T community read and speak languages other than English. We demonstrate by our actions that we know little of the folkways, mores, religions, or values — let alone the spoken tongues — of our foreign competitors and collaborators. When will the community awaken to this present global reality?

I am all for continuing Shapley's and Roy's goal of stimulating and focusing debate on the health and national contribution of our science and technology establishment. I particularly urge stretching the time dimension of the debate further into the future. After all, the future is the only thing we can do anything about.

But the status quo will remain unless each of us takes some action beyond debating. And many people want to change the status quo, including many who may disagree with the Shapley and Roy theses and remedies. My proposals:

1. *Initiate research and experimentation on institutional innovation to improve the conduct and application of S&T for the benefit of society.* First there is the question of how to do it: i.e., the interactions, integration, synthesis, and language, as well as the problems of substance and process. Second, there is the question of the institutional locus, the role of the leader, incentives and rewards, conflict resolution, sponsor relations, etc. And if innovating with existing institutions is infeasible, why not build new ones for the next generation? Shapley and Roy say: "let us start with a clean slate," after all.

2. *Build a Lost at the Frontier Network.* Identify as many full or partial supporters of the Shapley and Roy theses as possible and make them known to one another. Networking is an efficient way of organizing. Networks are cheap, easy, fast, and fluid. Nor are networks new to scientists, engineers, or science policy people. We call our existing ones "invisible colleges." Even though this network may be initiated by a book or an event, it would emphasize person-to-person communication, first within the network and increasingly outside. The network is my substitute for the authors' proposed advisory board.

Two don'ts regarding the network: (1) Don't formalize it with someone in charge: leaders and followers should change with groupings of participants. (2) Don't propose that the National

Science Foundation award a peer-reviewed grant to write the network's report. If it works, there will be no need for a report. Anyway, the scientific "peers" reviewing the proposal would trash the idea.

3. *Write a Science—The Endless Frontier, II, as a national science policy.* The 1976 National and Technology Policy, Organization and Priorities Act mentioned earlier is a dated *de jure* national science policy, and we certainly have an unsatisfactory *de facto* one. Why not write a better one for the 40th anniversary of *Science—The Endless Frontier* on July 5, 1985? However, unlike in the original Bush report, *all* parties to the science-and-society contract should participate in the new one and the resulting action documents should reflect their consensus—not partisan propaganda. Proposed actions should be directed not at ill-defined parties but at the signers themselves.

NOTES

[1] A major implementation of the foresight provision was the publication by the House Science and Technology Committee, *Survey of Science and Technology Issues: Present and Future* (Serial G, June 1981). For a more comprehensive review of the science and technology foresight and assessment activities of the 1970s, see Walter A. Hahn, "Science and Technology and the American Congress—II," *The Parliamentarian*, Vol. 62, No. 1, January 1981, pp. 1–17.

[2] See, for example, Stanley M. Davis, "Management Models for the Future," *New Management*, Vol. 1, Spring 1982, p. 12.

[3] Walter A. Hahn and Timothy C. Biggs, "Congress and the Emerging Perspective of Science," House Committee on Science and Technology, Print Serial G, June 1981, pp. 411–416.

[4] These shifts are described, among other places, in Daniel Yankelovich's *New Rules* (Bantam, 1981); Robert Hamrin, *Managing Growth in the 1980s: Toward a New Economics* (Praeger, 1980); Orio Giarini, *Dialogue on Wealth and Welfare: An Alternative View of World Capital Formation* (Pergamon, 1980).

Response from • JAMES R. KILLIAN, JR.

James R. Killian, Jr., after serving in various positions on M.I.T.'s magazine *Technology Review*, became executive assistant to M.I.T.'s president in 1939. He became executive vice-president of that institution in 1943 and vice-president in 1945. He served as president from 1948 until he became chairman of the M.I.T. Corporation in 1959. He served in this capacity until he became honorary chairman and served as honorary chairman from 1971–1979. Dr. Killian was the first presidential science adviser, serving as special assistant to the President for science and technology under Dwight D. Eisenhower from 1957–1959 and on the President's Science Advisory Committee from 1957–1961.

As I write this commentary, I am engaged in the completion of a memoir covering my career as a science administrator, to be published by the M.I.T. Press under the title, *The Education of a College President*. I draw upon this record, particularly to show how M.I.T. has managed its cooperation with industry and how federal science policy aimed at encouraging the interdependence between basic and applied research, which I believe is essential.

I start in 1939, when I became Executive Assistant to President Karl Compton at M.I.T. Subsequently I experienced the introduction into M.I.T., in 1940, of the Radiation Laboratory by the National Defense Research Committee. This wartime experience was destined to grow in size to a population of nearly 4,000. It was Dr. Lee DuBridge, Director of this laboratory, who summed up its achievements by remarking that radar won the war and the atom bomb ended it.

In my role as assistant to Dr. Compton, I was able to observe how this remarkable laboratory demonstrated the effectiveness of integrated research, in which engineering and applied research were effectively marshalled, along with basic research, in the development of radar for war use. The success of the Radiation

Laboratory had a profound influence upon the future development of M.I.T. as a research university.

In 1944, professors at M.I.T., notably John Slater, were prompted to propose that M.I.T. take a leaf out of the Radiation Laboratory when it closed and establish an interdepartmental laboratory "to conduct research in the field of electronics in association with the Departments of Physics and Electrical Engineering." This recommendation of Slater's was approved, and the Institute's first interdepartmental, interdisciplinary laboratory was established (the Research Laboratory of Electronics). Its success in the ensuing years led to the establishment of other interdepartmental laboratories as, for example, in materials science and engineering. These aided the advancement and coherence of both basic science and applied science and, along with strong departments, contributed importantly to M.I.T.'s transformation into a research university where basic and applied research marched together.

In materials prepared for the accreditation team of the New England Association of Schools and Colleges in 1979, M.I.T. included in its list of major laboratories, centers, and interdepartmental programs nearly forty organizational units associated with but not part of departments.

I come next to a description of an arrangement whereby M.I.T. sought to develop closer relationships with a selected group of industrial corporations who were prepared to make annual grants in support of the Institute and its research. The plan involved M.I.T.'s keeping corporations systematically informed about both pure and applied research done at the Institute, and maintaining a staff of liaison officers who would facilitate arrangements for company personnel to visit the Institute. In turn, M.I.T. personnel would visit the companies. This arrangement proved to be attractive to a growing number of corporations and worked in a way that was entirely acceptable to the faculty of the Institute; in fact the plan was shaped with faculty advice. Its success was demonstrated by the fact that, by 1984, the program had a membership of about 300 companies, and since its beginning has yielded a total of more than $70 million in corporate contributions to the Institute.

In 1957, I accepted an invitation from President Eisenhower to be his Special Assistant for Science and Technology to chair the President's Science Advisory Committee. This presidential advisory arrangement dealt with many matters on the President's agenda, including the outline of a national space program and specific recommendations for the transformation of the National Advisory Committee for Aeronautics into a civilian agency, the National Aeronautics and Space Administration, to administer our national space program except for those aspects directed to military objectives.

Among the PSAC panels appointed was a study of ways of strengthening American science which had been requested by President Eisenhower. Upon completing its study, this panel, chaired by Emanuel Piore, presented its conclusions to a full-dress meeting of the Cabinet and included a recommendation for the establishment of a council to be known as the Federal Council for Science and Technology. The President approved this recommendation, and it was in the discussions of this body that William O. Baker presented a persuasive report on the importance of the federal government's aiding in the establishment of a group of interdisciplinary centers in universities devoted to materials science and engineering. The new Council approved Baker's proposal, and happily, Herbert York, then in charge of the Advanced Research Projects Agency, arranged for funds to be made available by the Department of Defense. As a result, more than a dozen interdisciplinary centers for the advancement of research and learning in the fields of materials science and engineering were established in American institutions.

In making its report to the President and the Cabinet, the Piore panel included the following statement:

One of the clearest lessons to emerge from the history of science is that various scientific disciplines – seemingly unrelated – have a way of stimulating and fructifying each other in an unexpected manner. This complex back-and-forth interplay is the life and soul of science and technology – there can never be too much of it. The most impractical thing that can be done in designing and directing programs of scientific research is to worry overmuch about how "practical" they are.

In the early 1950s Professor Jerrold Zacharias led a program for curriculum reform for science teaching in high schools when he organized the Physical Science Study Committee (the "PSSC"), which undertook the development of a comprehensive program for the high school teaching of physics. This program was financed mainly by the National Science Foundation and in lesser amounts by other foundations and was a hinge program in bringing the universities into a new relationship with the teaching of science in pre-college schools. In this effort the National Science Foundation played a crucial role, and out of the demonstration of the successful impact of this program came the efforts for programs in biology, chemistry, and mathematics and programs for training a teacher to teach these new curricula.

The PSSC curriculum demonstrated that the university scholar and scientist, when motivated and provided with the means and leadership, could make a great impact on the quality of teaching in pre-college schools.

I have vivid recollections of two other assignments. The first was to participate in the preparation of a report of a Commission on National Goals, which had been proposed by President Eisenhower. Its 1960 report included an essay by Warren Weaver, "A Great Age for Science," which stands as one of the most eloquent statements that I know about the contributions of science to the national purpose. In speakng of the several kinds of research in that essay, particularly basic research and applied research, he said, "Both types of research are of the highest importance and it is silly to view one as more dignified and worthy than the other."

In 1959, the National Academy of Sciences, the American Association for the Advancement of Science, and the Alfred P. Sloan Foundation sponsored a Symposium on Basic Research. I had the happy experience of inviting President Eisenhower to be one of the speakers, and he accepted. In his summary of the symposium, Dael Wolfle emphasized that "the purpose of all scholarly activity, including research, is to develop the structure of knowledge. To this end, both applied and basic research contribute. Moreover, there is constant interaction and reciprocal fertilization between the two. Basic research provides a firm foundation for practical applications, and applied research may lead to beautiful basic science." His statement reflected the fact that the importance of applied research was stressed, along with that of basic research, in this symposium.

If in an increasing number of places applied research is tending to become a poor relation and is faltering, its association with basic research is one of the best ways to ensure its effectiveness, and, in turn, basic research gains from its close association with applied.

Response from • EDWIN H. LAND

Edwin H. Land, while a freshman at college, invented the first extensive synthetic sheet polarizer of light and, subsequently, a series of polarizers. Continuing to work on the theory and application of polarized light, he invented devices for automobile headlights and 3-D pictures. In 1937 he organized the Polaroid Corporation. In 1943 he conceived of the instant dry photographic camera, which led to a series of discoveries and subsequent developments. The black-and-white camera and film were first demonstrated publicly 3 years later. The one-step color process was demonstrated in 1960. Land holds the National Medal of Science and is a member of the National Inventors Hall of Fame, which includes Thomas A. Edison, Alexander Graham Bell, the Wright brothers, and others. In 1982 he retired as chairman of the board of Polaroid to be director of the Rowland Institute for Science and to continue his study of the theory of color vision. Since 1956 he has been a Visiting Institute Professor at M.I.T. Land has undertaken much public service, including being a member of one of the committees Vannevar Bush organized in 1944 to propose a postwar organization for U.S. science.

Many years ago, I tried to design a corporate environment that would embrace the whole range of activities: pure science, applied science, engineering, production. My hope was that the families of professions associated with these categories could coexist symbiotically. While we were successful to a remarkable degree, it is not clear to me that such a program is generally feasible. In my association with M.I.T. I had hoped to develop a program there that would train young people to lead and participate in such new corporate concepts. But those of us who might have organized it did not have the spare time to carry out such an ambitious undertaking. After all these years, I come to the following minimum conclusion.

We need to generate a modernized definition of engineering which would embrace all of the *application* of science. Pure science deals with the never-ending search for a better statement of its axioms, its premises, and with the new insights made possible by this search. Engineering must make do with the *product* of pure science, with both its fallacies and its truths. Neither the engineer nor the scientist can know what part of science at any moment is true and what part is fallacious. It is the task of the profession of "scientist" continuously to replace the fallacies with closer approximation to the truth. It is the task of the profession of "engineer" to use science as it stands. Both professions require talent, training, and inspiration. Occasionally a person may be a member of both professions but even then only if the person has the competence for a change in character and outlook as he turns from the one profession to the other. It is only if this major distinction between the two professions is kept in mind that one should encourage a shotgun marriage between the two domains. If the distinction is indeed maintained, then a consanguinous relationship can bring to the engineer a poetic sense of the significance of his own process for applying science, and to the pure scientist a deep satisfaction in seeing the product of his theoretical-experimental domain established in the operative world around him.

I recall that many of us on the Bush committee 40 years ago felt that both the inspired scientist and the inspired engineer were at that time at least relatively rare. One of our principal purposes was to help discover them and support them. I sometimes feel that the very success of technology has brought such a vast population into its domain that it may be particularly difficult to isolate these relatively few people who are naturally inspired; therefore it is difficult to locate the ever more significant contribution of our science and engineering in the midst of countless necessary but relatively unexciting undertakings. Nevertheless, I am convinced that there are more great people than ever before doing greater work than ever before. While I feel optimistic, it is not clear to me just how the hopes I had then for a continuum between science, engineering and production can be implemented in today's industrial structure.

The paper that follows, though from 1965, reflects my views on the task of establishing integrated science-engineering-production companies.*

* Taken from the Charles F. Kettering Award Address delivered 17 June 1965.

For many years I have been interested in the question of how to establish in the United States a large number of new companies based in science. My dream was that each of these companies would conceive of a new field and would carry on from the basic scientific work in that field through research, development, engineering, production, aesthetic design, lively, honest advertising, and efficient distribution. I still believe in that dream. The case histories from our own experience of the inventive process may offer insight into how to encourage such companies as I seek.

As I review the nature of the creative drive in the inventive scientists that have been around me, as well as in myself, I find the first event is an urge to make a significant intellectual contribution that can be tangibly embodied in a product or process. The urge, as pure urge, precedes in a perfectly generalized way the specific contribution — so that the individual hunts for a *domain* in which to utilize the urge.

The early stage need not be early in life, it can occur intermittently throughout life. The hunting process is fascinating to contemplate because during it there may be many abortive first approaches at the verbal level to fields which are then rejected — and then, quite suddenly, a field will emerge conceptually so full blown in the creator's mind that the words can scarcely come from his mouth fast enough to describe the new field in its full implication and elaborateness.

This domain, which neither he nor the world had known until some magic moment, now is for him so vividly real and well populated with ideas and structures that he will lead you around through it like a guide in a European city. Then it appears to him that all that is left to do is to parallel that intricate "reality" which came into being in his mind, with a corresponding reality in the world outside of his mind. Sometimes this process of creating the outside reality may take 5 years, sometimes 5 hours. For the creative person this process of establishing the correspondence between the outside reality and the one within his mind is a timeless undertaking, reminiscent of the relativistic trips through space in which people return to earth only a little older, while the rest of mankind has aged.

Whether the process is the 5-hour process or the 5-year process it always turns out to be true that many subsidiary and supporting inventions and insights are required to go from the thing in the mind to the thing in the world. These subsidiary inventions are born of accurate analysis, patient research, broad experience, and total devotion to the perfection of the outer reality.

This kind of timeless life can be lived only in an appropriate environment, a different kind of environment from what we must establish for some of our important massive engineering undertakings, such as the moon probe, undertakings in which a date must be met at all costs, and in which individual profundity must be largely displaced by rapid fire interaction between brilliant members of large groups. Since it is somewhat easier for the general public to understand and for the government to manage this latter type of intellectual activity, we must be extremely careful to nurture and protect the former type.

I can still recall the full vividness of my own need at the age of seventeen to do something scientifically significant and tangibly demonstrable. At the age in which each week seems like a year, I picked field after field before I decided that the great opportunity was polarized light.

Jumping ahead 17 years, I recall a sunny vacation day in Santa Fe, New Mexico, when my little daughter asked why she could not see at once the picture I had just taken of her. As I walked around that charming town I undertook the task of solving the puzzle she had set me. Within the hour, the camera, the film, and the physical chemistry became so clear to me that with a great sense of excitement I hurried over to the place where Donald Brown, our Patent Attorney (in Santa Fe by coincidence), was staying to describe to him in great detail a dry camera which would give a picture immediately after exposure. Only 3 years later, 3 years of the timeless intensive work referred to above, we gave to the Optical Society of America the full demonstration of the working system.

What is hard to convey, in anything short of a thick book, is the years of rich experience that were compressed into those 3 years. It was as if all that we had done in learning to make polarizers, the knowledge of plastics, and the properties of viscous liquids, the preparation of microscopic crystals smaller than the wavelength of light, the laminating of plastic sheets, living in the world of colloids in supersaturated solutions, had been a school and a preparation both for that first day in which I suddenly knew how to make a one-step dry photographic process and for the following 3 years in which we made the very vivid dream into a solid reality.

We can see the signficance of environment, of a corporate life whose managerial center was concerned with scientific ideas — a corporate life in which everyone participated in the mastery day by day of the new technological problems that arose in our search for better polarizers and new ways of using them. The transfer from the field of polarized light to the field of photography was for us all a miraculous experience, as if we had entered a new country with a different language and different customs, only to find that we could speak the language at once and master the customs. In short, the kind of training we had given ourselves in the field of polarized light had endowed us with a competence we had not sought and did not know we had; namely, a competence to transfer what must be a common denominator in *all* honestly pursued research, from one field to an entirely different one.

I am inclined to think that only in a corporation, however small or large, in which individuals are expected to make the center of their life the intellectual life of the laboratory can this kind of transferable talent be built. This process must continue for year upon year and decade upon decade. I find men around me in our laboratory who have lived this way and who now seem more alert, creative, and productive than when they were 30 years younger. That creativity is tied to some youthful age is a myth that comes about, I believe, because for one reason or another men stop living this way, perhaps because they are encouraged to think that there is more dignity associated with tasks implying power over people than with tasks implying power over nature.

Remember that we are searching these case histories not for the purpose of intimate revelation, but to try to find out why more scientific companies do not survive. Whatever the other reasons may be, I think that a primary reason is that at just the time when

Scientific creativity. (SOURCE: Nalimov, p. 39.)

a man's talent might be maturing, he is drawn off into a variety of so-called managerial activities. It is impossible for the long, long thoughts, the profound thoughts, the unconscious accumulation of insights, to come into being after these serious digressions into management. In most of the worthwhile problems, so many variables are involved that the human mind cannot keep them in order in the presence of interruptions. It is simultaneous mastery of a hundred interacting variables that is the glory of the kind of scientist we are talking about for our scientific companies.

When I started on the actual program of making the black-and-white film for our camera I set down the broad principles that would also apply to color. I invited Howard Rogers who had worked with me for many years in the field of polarized light to sit opposite me in the black-and-white laboratory and think about color. For several years he simply sat and, saying very little, assimilated the techniques we were using in black-and-white. Then one day he stood up and said, "I'm ready to start now." So we built the color laboratory next to the black-and-white laboratory and from then on until the time many years later when we released our color film, the program of matching the dream of the color process that was in our mind with the reality of the color process in the outside world never stopped. My point is that we created an environment, in which a man was *expected* to sit and think for 2 years.

You will note that the qualities that I am concerned about in corporate life are not related to bigness or smallness as such. There are small companies and small businesses that are not oriented towards thoughtfulness and profundity, and there are a few large corporations in which they are encouraged. But our universities do not train for patient and extended thought, and those few areas in government which have provided thoughtful environments are in certain danger of being swamped by the great mass undertakings. During the period ahead of us, many of us will be working to invent methods whereby the government can catalyze the formation and growth of creative companies. We shall also be trying within the universities to generate men with competence for profound individuality.

Response from • **F. JAMES RUTHERFORD**

F. James Rutherford is Chief Education Officer, American Association for the Advancement of Science. A former science teacher in the South San Francisco High School, teachers' association president, and public library trustee, he was a designer of some of the science curricula developed by the government in response to Sputnik in 1957. Among other positions, he has served as Assistant Director for Science Education of the National Science Foundation (1977–1980) and as Assistant Secretary of Education for Educational Research and Development of the Department of Education.

We seem to be the victim of our dichotomies. Shapley and Roy have made a strong case that by separating science into two classes, "basic" and "applied," valuing the one over the other, and failing to recognize fully the intrinsic interdependence between them, we have endangered our scientific future and stand to fail the nation. I would suggest that to view "research" and "education" as entirely separate and competing domains is detrimental to science, education, and the nation. All too often we who are within the fold glorify science while deploring and ghettoizing the field of education.

I would not claim, nor do Shapley and Roy, that science is one big bowl of porridge in which every spoonful is like every other. Basic research, purposive basic research, applied research, engineering, and technology are operationally distinguishable from one another and warrant separate attention and resources. But in the long run, no one of them stands alone or is of greater significance than the others, for it is the interaction among them that yields the greatest payoff to society and justifies its investment. In the same sense, scientific research, the training of future scientists and engineers, and the education of the public in science and technology are all interconnected, reinforcing parts of the scientific enterprise. Neglect one, and you impede them all.

201

In this brief response, I will not attempt to defend the claim that our practice of treating science education as though it were outside the house of science hurts science and the nation. I will assume it to be so and propose a few remedies, based on my experience as a designer of high school science curricula after Sputnik and as a former assistant director of the National Science Foundation for education.

My starting position is that no coherent national science education policy now exists, and the country needs to formulate one. I am not among those who oppose national education policy for ideological reasons; nor do I think such a thing is impractical. But in some ways the idea of a national policy for science education is hard to come to terms with. Decisions big and small are made all the time that relate to the teaching of science. They are made by legislators, bureaucrats, adminstrators, school board members, city council members, business executives, college professors and admissions officers, and teachers. These decision-makers are to be found in 50 state capitals, 16,000 school districts, hundreds of regional educational entities, 3,000 colleges and universities, many public and private organizations, and tens of thousands of communities. This *potpourri* of decisions determines what kind and quality of science education the nation will have.

Now, although these decisions are made largely independent of one another, oddly enough, the result appears to be lock-step science education, for the pattern of content, methodology, standards, time, resource allocation, student response, etc., is dispiritingly the same across the land. Therefore much must happen, in many places, for significant change to occur in science education in our nation.

The only real chance we have to get the state and local change vectors headed in the same general direction for long enough is for the federal government to assume a strong leadership role. I do not mean that it should seize control of science education, but that an explicit package of federal policies be the lynchpin and guide for local decision-makers. For only the federal government can continually clarify where we are, as a nation, in science and math education. Only the federal government can afford to provide for the continuing future of education in the sciences by being able to develop curricula and to undertake research to continuously improve what goes on in the schools.

Federal policy needs to incorporate two principles.

- *Science education should be viewed as an integral part of science.* This calls for the policy to develop as one part of an overall national science policy, not as an embellishment, afterthought, political sop, or separate "house" of its own.
- *Science education should portray science in its fullness.* Drawing on Shapley and Roy, this means that science education ought not to teach that basic science is independent of and superior to applied science, engineering technology, and the utilization of science in society. Shapley and Roy make this case for science policy; I support a parallel case for science education policy.

The National Science Foundation is the logical agency to be required to produce a far-reaching action plan to implement national science education policy. This would amount to no more than implementing its original mandate, in paragraph one of the legislation founding the agency, which gives the National Science Board the mandate to "develop and encourage the pursuit of a national policy for the promotion of basic research and education in the sciences." This mandate has never been given to the Department of Education (DOE) nor to the National Institute of Education (NIE). Moreover, the function should not reside in DOE, which is primarily concerned with transferring funds in block grants to states and student loans programs. NIE would be a wrong home for this function because, while it funds some research on learning, it is not connected to or concerned directly with the nation's scientific and technical cutting edge, which needs to be the driving force in improving science education.

The renewal of NSF's mandate in science education should aim to make education comprise one-third of that agency's budget within a decade. Also:

- The National Science Board should include experts in science education, just as it has come to include engineers, and social scientists. Presidents of universities or deans of engineering do not automatically qualify as experts in science education for the general public.

• NSF should help put programs in place covering every level of science, mathematics, and engineering education from preschool through postdoctoral, formal and informal.

• There should be a mechanism for informing the nation periodically and cogently on its performance in science education, the way periodic reports of the NSF and the National Academy of Sciences update how we are doing in basic science.

• Research and development should be undertaken on how best to teach science at each level. A priority of this research should be how to achieve widespread scientific and technological literacy, a goal which should lead NSF to support innovative curriculum development as it did after Sputnik, but, this time, to stick with it.

In the context of the issues raised by Shapley and Roy, I would suggest that two of their recommendations for stabilizing U.S. research and increasing its productivity be applied to R&D in science education. Transposed, they are:

• Long-term funding should be provided to high-quality specialists or teams for research and development in science education. This is especially important to induce high-quality people to spend a sizable fraction of their time over 5 years or more. It is also important to make up for the reluctance of academic scientists and engineers (particularly young people seeking tenure in traditional disciplines) to invest themselves in educational matters at the possible expense of their "real" research. Such funding, in time, could build up a national resource of top-flight contributors to guide ongoing reform of U.S. science education.

• Create a small number of science education R&D centers. Some might be in universities, others in industry or within scientific societies. Still others might be free-standing organizations. Each would have a critical mass of professionals drawn from academe, industry, and the educational system. Support would come from NSF and other public and private sources and from the return on its own products. Perhaps even the existing, big national laboratories could be organized on behalf of long-term national science education objectives. All of these could, in the process, build a distinguished place for education in the house of science.

Response from • ERIC A. WALKER

Eric A. Walker is a former President of the National Academy of Engineering (1966–1970) and former President of The Pennsylvania State University (1956–1970). An electrical engineer working in the field of underwater acoustics, he played a key role in the development of the underwater homing torpedo among other things. Walker received the Horatio Alger Award in 1959 and, among other posts, is currently Chairman of the Board of the Institute for Defense Analyses.

Here is the engineers' side of the story.

Several historical factors gave U.S. engineers second-rate status after World War II. In the late 1940s and 1950s, most of the science policy-making people in the government were scientists: physicists, chemists, and biologists. Engineers in American industry got into the war 3 years before the scientists were called upon to play any part. American industry was providing matériel for the allies, and most of this matériel was being provided on an order basis. "We want so many of this kind of airplane, so many of this kind of tank, and so many ships." These were not new designs; they were made after designs that already existed. So American industry put most of its engineers to work not on research, but on development, and principally on manufacturing. Also, as the student bodies of engineering schools dried up with people going into the services, many of the engineering professors, and certainly the best of them, went into industry, and followed their industry predecessors into the manufacturing, development, and improvement of weapons. Thus, when America got into the war, there was not a large cadre of unemployed engineers.

Thus, it happened that when America entered the war and the Office of Scientific Research and Development (OSRD) was formed, its head, Vannevar Bush, had to draw on the people who were not already employed in war work. These were mostly the people engaged in basic research in the physics, mathematics, and chemistry departments of our universities. Therefore, they were called upon to staff the central offices of the OSRD and to put together the laboratories in universities which were to develop and design new weapons.

When the war began to wind down, it did just that. It wound down, rather than stopping suddenly. Before the capitulation of Germany, American industry could see that soon the demand for weapons would dry up. So it moved people into research and development on new products needed to sustain the companies in peace. Simultaneously, there was a tremendous demand for engineering teachers as the GIs came home, because so many of those discharged wanted to go into engineering and other branches of technology. So almost immediately the technologists found employment either in industry or in education.

At the war's close, there was no such immediate outlet for the academic scientists. They had few graduate students to train in the universities and industry did not start up its basic research laboratories until later. So they had to find sources of funds to carry on their research. Moreover, a number of scientists found themselves employed at universities which would no longer engage in secret research. Having had their fill of war research, they decided to go back into basic research. Some even claimed they were going into "pure" research, as if all other kinds of research were impure. Because the leading scientists did this, many of the lesser-lights followed suit: it became almost a fad to claim one was doing pure research. One of my physics professors once proudly told me that no one could find a use for his research, it was that pure.

So they had to mount a campaign to get money for research in the universities, and their cry was, "look at all the benefits that we got from research done during the war." This was not quite true; although research had pointed the way, the benefits came from development and engineering. But this was a fact that they did not care to bring up. Further, when the military began to find people for the Defense Science Board, for the naval research advisory committee, and when the National Academy of Sciences wanted to staff committees on undersea warfare (the mine warfare committee, the radar committee, and others), the scientists, i.e., the basic researchers, were available and got the jobs. The result was that engineering and technology were pretty much shut out of these councils. Government laboratories of the Department of Defense, the Atomic Energy Commission, and organizations such as the National Science Foundation were staffed mostly by scientists, not engineers.

The years since have been the continuation of the abysmal misunderstanding of many scientists as to who engineers are and what they do. Scientists dismiss engineers with the statement that "of course, science includes engineering." This was the attitude which did us wrong when the National Science Foundation Act was passed and funded. Originally it had been intended that there would be a National Science and Engineering Foundation, but the word "engineering" got lost in committee hearings and the markup of the bill. The omission was condoned by the familiar cry, "of course, everyone understands that science includes engineering." Indeed, many scientists do think of engineering as another science, a kind of astronomy or biology or one of those other sciences (with which I am not very familiar).

But the difference between science and engineering is very real, as every engineer knows. Scientists are in search of knowledge; they don't determine where their investigations will go. The results of one step determine what next step to take. And so they develop new facts, new laws, and new understandings. But the engineers are the ones who take those understandings to design, develop, and make the artifacts or systems the public wants and for which it is willing to pay. There is no such thing as "pure" engineering. The goal is a product, and the product determines what one does in order to develop it. Unfortunately, even today, when engineers submit proposals they are judged by scientists and refused with the excuse that "this investigation will not add to our basic understanding." The scientists would forget that engineering is not supposed to lend to basic understanding. The purpose of engineering is to produce something that people want. Therefore engineers were left out of the NSF. There used not to be an engineering division in the NSF and the funds devoted to engineering during its first 10 years were minuscule by any measure. And ever since the creation of the engineering division, the underlying anti-engineering bias has not changed.

As a result of this discrimination, and probably because of other intangible factors, engineers individually and as a community developed an inferiority complex. Most engineers, when they became famous or prominent or solved an important problem, found themselves being called scientists, and were secretly pleased with this title. James A. Michener in *Space* repeats this comment: "A great breakthrough is a scientific triumph, a failure is an engineering failure. A spectacular technical feat is a scientific success, and engineering is never mentioned, even though it is done by engineers, is operated by engineers, and was designed by engineers."

Consequently, there was a great attraction to the idea of forming a National Academy of Engineering (NAE). Although there had been a National Academy of Sciences for nearly 100 years, and many said "of course, science includes engineering," this view was not borne out in the Academy's membership. There were a few, a salting of engineers. But only a few were elected and these because of their scientific rather than their engineering achievements. (In addition, few engineers are proposed for membership by members of the American Academy of Arts and Sciences, for the same reasons.)

There were other factors, too, which led to the formation of the NAE. The engineers felt they were unrecognized, that they never received attention in the press, and that they could not reach the high school students to tell them of the possibilities of engineering careers. It was *science* that hit the press, *science* that attracted the high school students, and *science* that had the status with the public. Although engineers had active engineering societies, these were effective mostly in disseminating technical information among member engineers. They kept their peers informed but had no contact with the general public or the press.

The engineers tried to remedy their perceived inferiority to the scientists, of course. There was a continuous parade for more than 50 years of "umbrella" societies which were supposed to fill these needs, but none had much success, because preexisting engineering societies were unwilling to give up their autonomy, or even cooperate. It became apparent that something new was needed.

So started the engineers' effort to form a prestigious organization where distinguished engineering achievement would be recognized. Of course, the minute the engineers showed signs of going it alone, the scientists said, "We still can gain something by cooperation." Some of the NAS scientists were willing to cooperate by changing the academy's rules. But in general, the NAS as an organization was not. On the other hand, some engineers felt that there was much to be gained by association with the scientists. "If we set up a wall between us, we will both lose," they said. So a joint committee was established. The then-president of the NAS tried to work towards an Academy with scientists and engineers as equal partners. Subsequent officers thought differently and the partnership became unequal; the engineers remained second-class citizens.

When it was formed, the NAE should have sought a federal charter of its own. The NAS specifically asked it not to because "then the Congress might reexamine the NAS's charter and change it to the detriment of all of us." Instead, having been born as a child of the NAS, the NAE soon found it was a stepchild. It did not have proper access to the appointment process for the committees of the National Research Council, and it could not appoint staffs of the committees. The NAS was the contracting officer and publisher. Fortunately, in the last few years the NAE is finally turning the tide with the rest of the technical community.

This still leaves public recognition to be attained. How can we reach the press, the general public, the high school students and their counsellors? I suggest that we work with the American Association for the Advancement of Science, especially if it can be renamed the American Association for the Advancement of Science and Engineering. That organization has solved the problem of getting press recognition and public attention. The engineering section of the AAAS has only 5,840 of the organization's 136,000 members. Only if the AAAS makes a major effort to show its interest in engineering will engineers join in sufficient numbers to bring their profession the recognition and public prestige it deserves.

Index

211